Dreamers Ink

A Journey of Discovery,
Forging Past the Obstacles and Storms in Life,
Into Our Dreams, Destiny, and Purpose!

Winning Our Race!

written by
Joseph James

published by
VaryMedia

© 2019 All Rights Reserved.
Reproduction in Whole or Part Without Written Permission is Prohibited. Printed in United States of America. Front cover and interior graphics designed by Joseph James for Dreamers Ink.

"Scripture quotations taken from the Amplified® Bible (AMP), Copyright © 2015 by The Lockman Foundation Used by permission. www.Lockman.org"

ISBN: 978-0-9982212-8-1

Dreamers Ink™
Joseph James
11844 Bandera Rd. #470
San Antonio, TX 78023, USA.

Visit us at:

Joseph-James.net | DreamersInk.net
SentencedToDeathDestinedForLife.com

CONTENTS

	Acknowledgments	vii
	Introduction	ix
Chapter 1	What is Dreamers Ink?	13
Chapter 2	What Are Dreams?	21
Chapter 3	Dreamers	27
Chapter 4	The Enemies Of Dreams	37
Chapter 5	Defining The Dream	49
Chapter 6	When A To B Is Not A Straight Line	55
Chapter 7	Real Dreams Are Not Selfish	65
Chapter 8	Dreamers Change Generations	73
Chapter 9	Kingdom Perspective	79
Chapter 10	On To Your Adventure	87
Chapter 11	Study Guide	95
	From The Author	115
	Resources	119

Acknowledgments

I am honored to have lived the life I have. Do I have regrets? Yes, a few, but not as many as I had originally thought, especially when I was younger. In some things I wish I would have made better choices, however, from the things I've discovered and the relationships that formed through these challenges, it has all been very instrumental in getting me to where I am today. If I were to go back and make some changes, it would obliterate a few precious lives very dear to me and I couldn't do that.

I am truly appreciative of all who have had an influence in my life, both good and bad. I've taken from that which was good and applied it to my life. I've also observed what was not so good and made a point to avoid that in my life.

There are many out there who proclaim they know the truth and they have an insatiable desire for others to follow them. I have come to the realization over the years that there is only one I can truly follow, Jesus Christ. We each can have a part of the truth when we follow the One who is the Truth. I am grateful to the many mentors and friends who have been in and are currently in my life. There are too many to list here, but some of the lessons I've learned from them are included in this book. Most of what I've shared is from my personal walk with the Lord and the revelations He's given me, especially in regards to dreams.

One of my favorite scriptures the Lord gave me in my youth is this:

1 John 2:27, "As for you, the anointing [the special gift, the preparation] which you received from Him remains [permanently] in you, and you have no need for anyone to teach you. But just as His anointing teaches you [giving you insight through the presence of the Holy Spirit] about all things, and is true and is not a lie, and just as His anointing has taught you, [c]you must remain in Him [being rooted in Him, knit to Him]."AMP

To my immediate family, my wife Janiece, my daughters Desiree, Krystal, and Lauren, and my son Daniel, all my grandchildren and those yet to come, thank you for your patience and grace in walking this journey with me. I hope that my life can be an inspiration in helping us all get closer to Him. I've made a lot of bad choices in my pursuit to find the truth. The main inheritance I want to leave with you is a clean generational bloodline with some great foundations to build your life upon. I didn't have that and it is so important to me to leave that to you. It is my hope and prayer that you build well.

To the rest of my family and my friends, thank you for your friendship, your help, your insight, and your encouragement along the way. I have learned so much on this journey, this wonderful road called life. It has been a true honor to have been a part of your life and I look forward to meeting new folks who will become new friends.

I want to give a special thanks to William Adkins, Rosanne Dolton and Michelle Still for their ideas and comments to help me adjust the manuscript to what it is now. Thank you to my son, Daniel, who edited the book.

JOSEPH JAMES

Introduction

Those who are pursuing their dreams search through all kinds of information that can help them in their quest. It can become an exciting adventure to discover the hidden things inside of us. Sometimes truth is hidden in various places and it takes a lot of searching to find it. In our search we throw out that which won't work for us, or place on a shelf for later review that which we're not sure about. I believe that while this book is written from a Christian perspective, there is a lot of information in it for everyone to glean something that might help them in their journey. I've read numerous books from lots of sources in my lifetime that have helped me get to where I am now. There are certain truths and principles that have been proven, like gravity for instance. It doesn't matter if you believe it to be fact or not, if one jumps off of a mountain without any gear to fly, they will fall. Just because they didn't believe in it doesn't change the fact that it's real. It is my hope that my perspective won't be a turn off to those who are seeking to find their dreams but don't believe the same way. I've written it in a fashion so that it can be read by all, simply skip over the portions you might disagree with or set them aside for perhaps a later time.

Over the last 30 plus years, I've been privileged to write many songs and some poems as well. It is truly a gift that I value greatly. In 1988, I bought a small sound system and a guitar to help a friend with praise and worship. A few weeks later songs were coming to me. I could literally write some of them in as little as fifteen minutes. As a writer I know that is a gift given to me because it just comes naturally. I love music. It has the capability to change not only our world, but generations to come. I began writing books in 1992.

I hope that this book blesses you, gives you a deeper understanding of His Kingdom, and compels you to go on and experience all that Father desires for your life. To those who don't believe in the Lord, I challenge you to read this book anyway and see what you discover in it. The contents might surprise you. Perhaps some of what you think you know, might not be what you discover as you read. Who knows, you might pick up a few things that will help you in your walk. I glean things from folks I disagree with on an ongoing basis, adding to my knowledge and wisdom.

This book encompasses excerpts from my life's journey, it's successes as well as failures that have helped form me into who I am today. Truly, without the valleys I've walked, the mountain tops wouldn't have had the meaning they do.

I'm sitting here right now at a Panera Bread restaurant in Colorado Springs looking out of the window at the mountains as I write, admiring Father's majestic creation with all of it's dangers and beauty. As the sun sets behind the mountains, it's the clouds in the sky, you know those things we might see as obstacles, light up with various colors giving us a magnificent view as another day comes to a close. Without a few clouds in the sky we wouldn't have the magnificent beauty of a sunset or sunrise and that's also true in our lives. We know that He is with us through the night as the stars and moon give us their light. Then as we dream in our sleep, a new day begs to start afresh. Our passion to go forward into the unknown chomps at the bit to begin a new day on this wonderful journey. What adventures will we face? Sometimes our dreams and visions in the night give us a clue. Here's to your adventure!

JOSEPH JAMES

Red Rocks Amphitheater | Denver, CO | Some day I want to play my music here. Dreams!

Helen Hunt Falls | Gold Camp Road | Colorado Springs, CO | Such a beautiful place to hike!

Chapter 1

What is Dreamers Ink?

DREAMERS INK is more than just a book, gift set, project, or concept. It is an actual journey, or even a way of life if you will. It's a path not only of defining and realizing our hopes and dreams, but helping others along the way to theirs. When we understand that the fulfillment of our dreams is dependent on the help and the interaction with others down our path, then we will have a different focus on how we all connect to help bring fulfillment to others dreams as well as our own. We are interconnected and not simply islands in this sea of humanity. So…

Let's take a journey together and discover a path we might not have seen yet or one that we might have simply walked on by in our life at one time or another. In my first book which is an allegory, DESTINY PATH OF LIFE | THE JOURNEY BEGINS, the main character rushes toward his dream on his way to a town called Journeytown and almost misses the most important part of the journey. The man, who interrupts his journey, has a key that he will desperately need soon to open some doors in the journey ahead. Will the dreamer pause and choose to spend enough of his valuable time to stop long enough to make a choice, the right choice, or will he pass it off as a delay, not that important, and just keep going? Are we watching for these things, or just blindly heading through life hoping we'll make it, or just hoping to get through each day.

In your choosing to read this book, it's clear to me that you are definitely searching for the truth, at least as far as it concerns you. What are these keys that will unlock doors in your path ahead?

I created DREAMERS INK because of the need I saw in our journey in helping others get through general life, depression, and suicide. In talking personally to thousands about the subject, it became clear that I needed to change my focus from a negative to a positive approach and proclamation. We've talked to many who were in one of the stages of depression or on the path to suicide. We've also worked to help those who have lost loved ones to suicide and to help them pick up the pieces. The Lord started speaking to me about a special tour at the end of 2015 and said that I should focus on the positive side of people's dreams, because everyone has had at least one dream in their life. So, we named the tour, FOLLOW YOUR DREAMS.

We moved out of our apartment and left San Antonio, Texas on a journey into the unknown in March of 2013 with our first destination being Colorado Springs, Colorado. Since then, this journey has taken us all over the USA numerous times, including a summer trip through Canada on the Alaskan Highway to Homer, Alaska…and back. (A bit of laughter here because it was a very long trip. We started in Texas and ended in Florida on that particular segment. Next time by plane or ship please!)

We've seen and experienced many different states, cities, communities, and cultures along the way. We've talked to folks and listened to their hearts. Some were caught in those deep and dark places and we tried to help them through. Some of them are still connected to us through various social media and other means. Some were the victims of suicide, left holding the tattered remains of a life gone too soon. The questions of 'Why?' haunting their souls and hearts. I became passionate and determined to find a way to be proactive from a positive stance and this is where DREAMERS INK comes in. It is the heart and core of our FOLLOW YOUR DREAMS Tour now. I am considering changing the tour to AMERICA DARE TO DREAM.

DREAMERS INK is something that anyone can do to help their loved ones, friends, peers, co-workers, and neighbors. It is something tangible that can be seen and focused upon as a daily reminder. It might just be a special ingredient to that individual's life.

I'm planning for DREAMERS INK to be a global connection and information group, formed to bridge the gap of hope and hopelessness in our country and worldwide. While we are based in a local community in the USA, a strategic base if you will, the internet allows us to connect globally to make a difference. No matter where we are presently and the circumstances we find ourselves, we can make a difference locally, regionally and globally. Everything starts with a dream/vision.

One of the key components of this endeavor is the DREAMERS INK Gift Set. Eventually, there will be at least five versions of this set from the original we are creating, with possibly more to come in the future. Of course, you don't have to purchase a set, you can simply make your own, but regardless, it would be of great benefit to have something tangible that you or your friends can see on a daily basis plus a journal to write in as well. The purpose behind the gift set is to help mentors, parents, and loved ones reach out to those around them in a tangible way to say 'we care' and 'we want to help'. It takes personal time to help someone define and write out their dreams with much needed encouragement and help along the way. There are too many bullies and naysayers out there who want to crush people's dreams for one reason or another. This can be individuals, groups, businesses, and those in power. We live in America - the land of dreams, and our own people are giving up and taking themselves out in the midst of temporary storms. If we can't fulfill our dreams in America, where can we? Millions of people are risking everything just to immigrate here for a chance to build a better life and to live their dream.

I want to take this a step further though. Perhaps through this project and group, these immigrants, instead of immigrating to America or another country, might become passionate enough to dare to create the same thing we have here in their own country, freedom. America stood up to England in the 1700's and gained our freedom and established a model for other countries. Many people gave their lives to establish this country and many since to protect and maintain it. This could be the time for change in other countries as folks begin to see how they can transform their country into a place of freedom and abundance.

In having said all of this, DREAMERS INK exists to help

What Is Dreamers Ink?

individuals, couples, and groups find their God-given dreams and then to encourage them to go for them. We endeavor to be part of the encouragement, denouncing bullying and the crushing of dreams through any form, to become a network of support through individuals, groups, businesses, etc., who want to help our fellow brothers and sisters fulfill their destiny and purpose in our generation and in the ones to come. By each individual realizing their dreams, the community, region, nations, and world will become a better place and morale will change along the way. I remember Martin Luther King Jr's. phrase, 'I have a dream!' He went on to change the world. It might cost us dearly and in his case his life, but regardless of what we do, wrong or right, the cost is great. There is no sitting on the fence and not being touched. One individual can change society and a generation, how much more can a bunch of us. We look around for heroes to lead the way, dare we look deep inside of us? Every hero is an ordinary person who made an extraordinary choice.

To help make all of this possible in the funding of our national and global outreaches, this book and the gift sets play an important role for individuals and groups to purchase. The following chapters will expound on this. There are basically five gift sets for a targeted audience, grade school, teens, young adults, adults, and professionals. The gift set includes its own specially designed box, case or pouch, a fountain/calligraphy pen of varying quality based on the targeted age maturity of the set, choice of ink colors, professional MY DREAM certificates designed on special paper for writing and displaying the dream (5-10 sheets), journal, and this book with the study guide in back. We might also include an optional frame at some point for the Dream Certificate to be mounted in a prominent place that can be seen everyday. It is hoped that the mentor or receiver purchase their own special frame(s), the design they want and then display it in a prominent place(s) to be constantly in view. I recommend making more than one copy and placing them in several places in the home and workplace, if possible. The more often we see it, the more it changes us inside until it becomes the focus. It also helps the isolated person think of the one who gave them the gift set, remembering in that instance of isolation and despair that they are not alone in the journey. Perhaps it will help them reach out in those moments of despair and/or hopelessness.

The main purpose of the gift set is for the giver to help their recipient start a journey in discovering who they are and why they are here. It is a journey of discovering identity and purpose in a world currently in chaos, seemingly without either. It is a journey of discovering our gifts and talents and then matching them with our passion and desire to win the race set out before us.

What Is Dreamers Ink?

Redwood Forest | California

Chapter 2

What Are Dreams?

*Merriam-Webster defines dream as, **"a strongly desired goal or purpose."***

Everything starts with a dream. Dreams give us a focal point as to the direction we want or need to take in our life. They are like planning a trip from Los Angeles to New York. We can start out in a general direction heading towards the northeast and then refine it along the way, course correcting as necessary. God started with a dream/vision and when it was completed, He proclaimed, "It is good. It is finished." In fact, Jesus shouted those same words from the cross, "It is finished!" thus testifying of the fulfillment of the plan for His crucifixion from the foundations of the earth. He also has a dream and purpose planned for each of us and, as a whole, for each and every generation on this earth.

Psalm 139:13-18, "For You formed my innermost parts; You knit me [together] in my mother's womb. 14 I will give thanks and praise to You, for I am fearfully and wonderfully made; wonderful are Your works, and my soul knows it very well. 15 My frame was not hidden from You, when I was being formed in secret, and intricately and skillfully formed [as if embroidered with many colors] in the depths of the earth. 16 Your eyes have seen my unformed substance; and in Your book were all written the days that were appointed for me, when as yet there was not one of them [even taking shape]. 17 How precious also are Your thoughts to me, O God! How vast is the sum of them! 18 If I could count them, they would outnumber the sand. When I awake, I am still with You. [AMP]

Jesus talked a lot about His Father's Kingdom and that it was at hand, near while He was here on the earth. Now, because of His sacrifice we can walk in His Kingdom too and advance it on the earth. Revelation chapters 2 & 3 talk about the responsibility of His body in each community/region. In His Kingdom everyone has a place and fits in according to where the Holy Spirit is placing them. Each of us has our own lane so there is no competition to see our race fulfilled and finished. The only thing that can stop us is if we choose to quit or run in a lane that's not ours. In a competition, if a runner runs in someone else's lane they are disqualified from the race. It is important that we find our race, our lane, and run to win. Even if we find ourselves in the wrong place or lane, we can stop, make adjustments, and get back on course. This is actually one definition of repentance; turn around and go back the other way. I think that one of the saddest moments could be when we get face to face with Jesus and we tell Him of all we've done and He opens our book and points to the plan He had for us that was totally different from ours. We ran someone else's race or something that wasn't really ours at all. Conversely, one of the happiest moments could be when we see Him and he shows us all of what we've accomplished in the book He wrote for us. Victory!

One thing we need to understand is that there are many

types of dreams. Some dreams are long term and some short term. Long term dreams generally last decades or a lifetime. Short term dreams might get us to a place where we can begin to see the long term dreams. Dreams generally change and adjust over time. This is why we provide multiple "MY DREAM" certificates in the DREAMERS INK gift set. If we can understand this at the beginning of our journey, we will avoid many disruptions and wasted time when we get to a crossroad or a roadblock. With this understanding, we can see that dreams are flexible, not as rigid as we might think, and that they can't really be broken, only adjusted or stretched. Occasionally, we will find that our dreams simply aren't big enough. The people that walk with us and the circumstances may change over time, but they are merely adjustments propelling us ever forward to our destiny. If we can understand this and keep it in our minds before us, we already have gained most of the victory.

Dreams are the motivation that keep us looking forward to the next day. There is hope built into them by design to help us keep looking forward in the discovering of the positive moments in each day. It is the passion in the dream that boost our energy levels and keep our bodies going even when we're tired. I like to look at it as similar to a treasure hunt. Being a Christian, I look for something special Father is placing in my day to encourage me. This is especially beneficial when the storms come or when it seems that everything is going backwards and in the wrong direction.

Yesterday, I went over to a friend's house with my Yamaha MOX8 keyboard, guitar, and sound system to practice. I hadn't been able to practice the keys in over 3 months because the three of us have been living in a hotel room. I got so discouraged at how many mistakes I was making. I left there really feeling down and on the thirty minutes drive back to our hotel I just asked the Lord to encourage me. I encourage others on a daily basis and some encourage me as well, but I wanted His encouragement, only from Him in this moment. I got back to the hotel and my wife was watching LA BAMBA, the Ritchie Valens story which encouraged me in seeing his struggle and success. I saw the number 777 on one of my apps a while later and some other small things at just the right time during the rest of the day. I knew Father was answering my cry. Music and singing has been a difficult journey for me because of all the negative comments I received as a child and the struggles along the way. So much fear was inside of me to ever believe my voice was good enough to sing. I've been writing and singing my music for 31 years now and sometimes it seems to go nowhere or at least not where I think it should go. Looking at my age and comparing myself to others around me can get quite discouraging at times. It's in those times though that the Lord's encouragement is paramount and I desperately need it. I love to be on stage and touch the hearts of those with my music and in speaking. To see their faces light up with new focus and hope is just incredible.

God-given dreams are always impossible for us to do on our own. In the dreams He has for us to accomplish, He has required a certain element that without Him CAN NOT be fulfilled. It's a simple word, but has embodied within it an incredible, supernatural power. This word is called His GRACE. It is empowered by His resurrection power. This power is the same power that raised Christ Jesus from the dead and it works within all of us who are born again. He's also designed our dream to be connected to others in order for it to be fulfilled. He just has this idea about the building of His Kingdom and He wants all of His people to be connected and to have a special place in it. His blessings can flow to each of us when we are all connected. Broken links cause the blessings to stop or to be interrupted. It's like the picture Ezekiel painted in Ezekiel 37, the Valley Of Dry Bones. We can not be an island to ourselves and hope to accomplish everything He has for us.

He showed me a lot of things as He gave me the words and visions to write my five-book series, ISLANDS IN THE SEA. I wrote each book from cover to cover over a span of nine years with each book bringing a new revelation. His Kingdom is connected and functioning across all generations and across all people in each generation. Time cannot separate it, nor stop it. The baton is handed down from generation to generation until His plan is finally completed. We can all be a part if we want, but the prerequisite is that we do it His way and be born again, in other words to invite Him into our heart and give us new life. He is the only One who knows the whole plan and who has the power to make it happen. He created us to enjoy the journey with Him, to discover all the wonderful and hidden things He's placed along our path. He wants to talk with us, to hear our thoughts, and He wants to share His heart and love with us, individually, and corporately. It's a wonderful journey of love.

MY CHILD

My child, did you see my painting in the morning sky?
It was just for you and I added a special touch.
Did you listen to my birds as they sang their songs of love?
Just wanted you to know, with joy, I'm singing over you.

Did you notice how My breath gently moved the leaves?
I wanted to touch your hair with the gentleness of My hands.
I know that you are busy and have so many things to do,
Yet, I know you're lonely and I would like to comfort you.

Will you give me a moment or two, just here and there?
I'll refresh your spirit and share some thoughts with you.
I watch you every day as I journey by your side.
Just wanting you to know you can always count on Me.

So, if you think about it, and could really use a friend,
Just take a moment and I will gladly listen in.
I want to hear your heart and I want to share My love.
'Cause really, You are the reason I am here.

I'll paint you another sunset as your day comes to a close,
To extend My peace and love, and refresh your weary soul.
If you're out in the dark at night, just look up at My stars,
And know I'm always watching, and want what's best for you.

As you look upon creation, and see the wonders in the sky,
Know it's My heart I'm sharing, in hopes that you reply.
My child, sometimes I'm lonely too and sure could use a friend.
Do you think we could meet real soon, and share this life of ours?

My child, I love you!
Father

© 2010 Joseph James

Chapter 3

Dreamers

In considering the dreams of many world and generation changers, Joseph's dream comes to mind. His story is found starting in Genesis 37. It is a typical story of a dreamer. Dreamers are sometimes full of pride, hated, but almost always mocked, diminished, and in some way tormented for dreaming something impossible to accomplish.

David's dream of becoming Israel's next king put him face to face with a giant, Goliath, who wanted him dead. One could argue that it wasn't his dream, but the Lord's dream and purpose. We don't know if David knew this before Samuel's prophesy when he anointed him, but we do know it was His God-given destiny. According to Psalm 139, which was written by David himself, his dream was written in heaven just like our book in heaven that the Lord has written for us.

What about our book though? How do we access it? How can we know Father's plan for our life? Is it a good plan? How much does He really care for us? What price will we have to pay with our lives? Well, let's just look at a few things briefly and perhaps we can get a better idea.

Jeremiah 29:11, *"For I know the plans and thoughts that I have for you,' says the Lord, 'plans for peace and well-being and not for disaster, to give you a future and a hope."AMP*

Hmmm! From the previous passage things really look bright for us if we can just see and/or hear what these plans are.

Psalm 139:13-18 "For You formed my innermost parts; You knit me [together] in my mother's womb. 14 I will give thanks and praise to You, for I am fearfully and wonderfully made; wonderful are Your works, and my soul knows it very well. 15 My frame was not hidden from You, when I was being formed in secret, and intricately and skillfully formed [as if embroidered with many colors] in the depths of the earth. 16 Your eyes have seen my unformed substance; and in Your book were all written the days that were appointed for me, when as yet there was not one of them [even taking shape].17 How precious also are Your thoughts to me, O God! How vast is the sum of them! 18 If I could count them, they would outnumber the sand. When I awake, I am still with You." AMP

Now we can see that He has a wonderful plan for our life and He wrote it all out in a book in heaven before we were ever born, most likely before the creation of the earth. In fact, it's possible our soul could have been in heaven while we were waiting for a mother and father to create a physical body for us to be placed into. Our soul is neither male nor female. Jesus referred to this (Matthew 22:30 & Mark 12:25). The body we were sent into is, and simply only that, to function together, male and female for procreation and for the Lord's purpose to be fulfilled. We were created in His image through Adam, separated into Adam and Eve, yet still a mirror of His image displaying the male and female sides of who the Lord is. In fact, in marriage the male and female are joined and become one again for the purpose the Lord has planned for them. Paul spoke a lot about this and also the marriage of Jesus to His Bride, the Church, of who we are a part of. In all of this, Paul talks about women showing the men how the Bride should interact with the husband, and men how Jesus interacts with His Bride so that they can be an example of His love, (Ephesians 5:22-33). Thus, we are not less of a being based on the physical body we are placed in, however, we do have a path to walk in conjunction with His dream for us. In all He has planned, His plan and destiny will fulfill our heart's yearning, passion, and desire, because He placed the dream there along with the necessary gifts and talents He's given each of us.

It says that He created everything in six days, so if our souls were not created in that time period then when, since He rested after that? It is possible that we could've even read this book, our own special book penned by His hand before we left heaven. Perhaps we were even all excited about the journey and destiny ahead, but then something happened. Being born as a baby into a physical world, we forgot all of what we had seen in heaven, perhaps that's why we see deja vues on occasion. Maybe it's glimpses into that spiritual realm. Who knows for sure. Could these be glimpses inside our book that we've seen before, but not while we were on this earth? Now that we are in this new body we find out we have choices on how we want to live. We can live according to that wonderful plan He wrote for us or we can try to do it our way. Sometimes the pull of desires from this fleshly body and its powerful urges, tries to steer us in a wrong direction that could bring harm to us. Our choice!

One could say that our soul came down from heaven and was placed into this wonderful body the Lord was creating for us in our mother's womb, according to Psalm 139:15. Jesus said that we would receive another body after our physical body dies and He proved it by walking among us in His new body after His resurrection. It must have been really different because even His disciples didn't recognize Him. At death, our soul and spirit leaves our physical body and is present with Him. Then we'll get another body, one that doesn't decay.

Then Psalm 139 goes on to say that there is a vast sum of precious and wonderful thoughts Father has towards us. In fact, the total number of those thoughts outnumber the sand. Can you imagine how long it would take to sit down with Father and listen to Him tell us individually of all of the wonderful thoughts He thinks about us? I mean, that number outnumbers the sand. I think it will take an eternity, but He tells us some of them every day, if we're listening.

Some say that Father is mean and mad at us, especially those who are very religious, those who are always trying to obey the law, trying to be perfect, as well as trying to get everyone else to be perfect too. I think differently on this. I believe that He loves us so much that He is constantly trying to encourage us and point us in the right direction so that we can stay safe and on the wonderful path He has for us. You see, if you really love someone you'll try to do everything you can to please them and make them happy. He does that with us and He knows that if we can see how much He loves us, perhaps we'll love Him enough to do the same with Him. Once we understand this everything else changes. Life becomes an adventure, one of discovery and hope instead of hopelessness and despair.

So now that we've talked some about dreams and a special plan for our life, why DREAMERS INK? Well, let's take a journey over to another book called Habakkuk. You see, Habakkuk was complaining to the Lord about all the wickedness that he was seeing in his generation and he saw that the wicked seemed to go unpunished for their part in it. After he is finished complaining, he sits back and waits to hear what the Lord has to say about it, knowing he might be reproved as well, but he still desperately wanted to know the answer. You can read the whole story if you want. I really like Habakkuk because his book gave me a revelation on how to talk to the Lord. I'll be expounding on this throughout the book, but here is a guy who has some questions, so he asks them and then the Lord gives him some insight. It is this kind of relationship that the Lord wants to have with each of us.

You see, Father is no respecter of people. If we ask Him, He will answer us on a need to know basis. This also applies to things for our personal lives like our book in heaven. Jesus said that if we ask for a fish He wouldn't give us a snake, or for bread, a scorpion. He desires to give us good things. He said to ask, seek, and knock and the door would be opened to us. The revelations or answers will be revealed. Sometimes it takes persistence and in that, persistence costs us something which is precious time. Time is something we value. In some instances, time is exchanged for money. Things that are free and easy sometimes don't mean that much to us and we tend to take them for granted.

The Lord has spread out a banquet table for us to enjoy.

There are many things on this table. The Lord says to taste and see that He is good, but what are we willing to taste?

In a banquet table here on earth there are many kinds of delicacies, some of which we might like and some not so much. We have the right to choose what we want, but do we choose a healthy diet? If all we do is eat meat, we will lack in other things and become deficient in some areas. Why not eat some from everything and maximize our experience and walk?

I picked up a lady at the Catholic church one day with the Lyft rental car. She said that her priest is trying to get people to raise their hands to the Lord when they sing. She said that she is from a strict Catholic background and doesn't like to do that. I told her it is her choice and asked her if she understood the significance of raising our hands. She said, 'no,' so I shared with her about spiritual warfare and what it does to the demonic realm when we raise our hands. Sometimes there can be a demonic cloud over us, a heaviness, oppression or depression, and when we lift our hands to praise Him our hands pierce that cloud and it dissipates. It's our physical hands, but it is also our spiritual hands because we are spirit beings as well. So we operate in both realms at the same time. It's not foolishness when we understand the revelation in it. Check out the many times this happened in the Bible and the results. We don't have to do this, but then we might not get the maximum effect in the victories we really want. These are things that are available on this banquet table. It is a table of revelations that can set us free, show us Who Father is, fill us with His love, and more. Aren't you a bit curious about what all is yours and available to you? All you have to do is eat, read about it, find out what is there and then apply it to your life. (Song of Solomon 2:3-6)

So, let's get back to the story. The Lord starts answering Habakkuk and tells him of the destruction that is coming by way of judgment because of all the wickedness of the people. It is going to take some time for it to come though, because the Lord doesn't want anyone to face judgment. He'd rather them turn from their wicked ways and come back to Him to receive mercy. This is a definition of repentance.

2 Peter 3:9, "The Lord is not slow in keeping his promise, as some understand slowness. Instead he is patient with you, not wanting anyone to perish, but everyone to come to repentance." AMP

*Habakkuk 2:1-3, "I will stand at my guard post and station myself on the tower; and I will keep watch to see what He will say to me, and what answer I will give [as His spokesman] when I am reproved. 2 Then the Lord answered me and said, "**Write the vision** and engrave it plainly on [clay] tablets so that the one who reads it will run. 3 'For the vision is yet for the **appointed [future] time** it **hurries** toward the goal [of fulfillment]; it will not fail. Even though it **delays**, wait [patiently] for it, because it will certainly come; it will not delay.'"AMP*

So, the vision/revelation needs to be written down. It's why we have the Bible we do, because the prophets and scribes were obedient to record what the Lord told them to write. Can you imagine a business owner trying to start a business without any type of business plan? How will others know what he is trying to do and what their part in it is unless it's written down so they can see? How can we see what a new invention looks like unless it is drawn or produced into a prototype? This is why we need to write down the dream.

Notice that one word though - delay - in verse three. I'm sure that's no one's favorite word by any means, definitely not mine, but He tells us plainly that it's going to take some time and that not everything might go as planned. In fact, there may be a few storms and rough patches along the way. He does tell us He will never leave us nor forsake us and will always be with us. The delay He is talking about though, will not keep the dream from happening.

We can plan to go to a party with a group of people. The plan is to meet up at a certain time and place to go together to the party. We might get there ahead of the others and have to wait, or delay until the others get there. It doesn't mean we'll be late, we're just waiting for everything to be in place.

What is the DREAMERS INK Certificate? It is a place to write down our vision or dream at this moment. Now, it doesn't mean that it's not going to change a bit or even look somewhat different as time goes on, but then again adjustments can be made as necessary along the way. Sometimes a little bit more maturity will change our view and understanding of what the Lord means by what He shows and tells us. We might actually be in a very delicate place when we get the original dream and can't handle some of the specific details at that point. Later on, we might be more healed and stronger to do some of the things necessary to go on which might have intimidated us before.

Perhaps we can create our own scrapbook, or mapping

so we can see our journey over the years to come. We can add each of these dream certificates to a book, on a computer program, or even hang them in order along a wall. Remember, it's our journey and we are free to do what we want with it. It might even encourage others to do the same when they see what we've done. Let it be an adventure and fun. Fun in the journey!

I didn't really discover my gift to write until I started writing songs in 1988. I was 26 at the time. So many young people are trying to understand their dream by the time they get out of high school. Sometimes we know a lot and sometimes we don't. We need to be okay with looking at it like an adventure that will take a lifetime with each day having some sort of encouragement and discovery in it.

The world system tells us we have to have it all figured out, hurry up, don't wait or it will pass you by. It tries to put us in its mold and control us. Rubbish! The Lord longs for us to walk in freedom and to discover His Kingdom and His ways. His way brings life and hope, the world's ways bring hopelessness and death. Choose wisely!

I WISH

I wish I could have grown up in the perfect family,
With a mother and father who love me so dearly,
With brothers and sisters who play instead of fight,
With each day a joyous adventure and peace through the night.

I wish I could have grown up in a world full of love,
One without wars, sin, grief, murder or strife,
Where it's safe to walk the streets and live in homes without locks,
Where everyone is full of love and each one like a friend.

This would be perfect, and then it would never end,
But in my world, a dream is all this will ever be,
Each one does his best just trying to make it through,
Yet, this one has the potential to be the greater of the two.

It's in these places, we find out if true love exists,
Without mercy and forgiveness, it's only shallow at best.
How can we know its depths if it's never tested and tried?
It only shines and glows when, by the storm, it's purified.

I thought there were many who loved me or so they did say,
But when the storms came, they ran off and went away.
"Where are you? I thought you were my friend."
But they were all gone when I had looked again.

"Where did you come from, I didn't know you were there?
I thought I knew everyone, but what is your name?"
"I am the Lord, and I've always been near,
I've never left you, you are precious and dear."

My tears fell like rain as I ran to embrace,
His love surrounded me and His peace and grace.
He is all I need, we're together each day,
He healed all my wounds, in His presence I'll stay.

Now, I have new friends and I know them by name,
I know their limits and failures and I love them the same.
Humans are fragile and weak at their best,
But Jesus is perfect and His love passes the test.

© 2011 Joseph James

Chapter 4

The Enemies Of Dreams

Joseph had a dream at the age of 17. He dreamed that his family and others would one day bow down to him. Little did he know what all he would go through to get to that place, but he ended up saving many lives because he never gave up no matter how bad it got and it got really bad. He got thrown into a pit by his own jealous brothers and sold into slavery. Then, as he was getting his life back together, he was falsely accused of sexual advances by his owner's wife and was thrown into prison, a dungeon. Ironically, when he was about as far down as he could get, it was his interpreting of dreams that released him into his destiny. He spent 13 years going through that difficult process and was 30 years old when he took over as second in command of Egypt with Pharaoh. *Genesis 37-41.* From that vantage point, after learning and maturing through all he had endured, he saved many people through a very bad famine that lasted for years. He was also there to save his family and in the end they did bow down to him as the dream had portrayed.

I'm sure there were many times he struggled with the dream. Perhaps there were many times he wished he could give up and possibly that he never had the dream in the first place. What did it all mean? How can it happen from this dark place in the dungeon? Will he ever see the light of day again? He was estranged from his family. He was innocent, yet he was placed among criminals. He continued to help others, but when they got free they forgot about him. How was he ever going to be able to get out of this prison, let alone dare to dream again? He didn't give up though. He kept going no matter what pictures of hopelessness were being painted in his mind before him. I wonder if he heard the words of his family mocking him. "Where is that dream now? Yeah, right!"

Proverbs 29:18, "Where there is no vision [no revelation of God and His word], the people are unrestrained; but happy and blessed is he who keeps the law [of God]." AMP

THE MENTAL SIDE: DEPRESSION & SUICIDE

There are many enemies of dreams. Some of them are timing, delay, broken relationships, culture, corporate structures, geographical locations, and the list goes on. These are all physical things that can occur along life's journey, but let's talk about some others as well.

<u>DEPRESSION</u>: *a state of feeling sad (Merriam-Webster)*

<u>SUICIDE</u>: *1. the act or an instance of killing oneself intentionally. 2. the self-inflicted ruin of one's own prospects (Merriam-Webster)*

THE JOURNEY FROM DEPRESSION TO SUICIDE

John 10:10, The thief comes only in order to steal and kill and destroy. I came that they may have and enjoy life, and have it in abundance [to the full, till it overflows]." AMP

Since Jesus came to give life in abundance, there is only one other that tries to stop it. He does this by trying to steal our hope. The longer he can delay our progress, the easier it is for us to lose sight of the vision/dream and start down a spiraling path from a spirit of heaviness, to depression, to hopelessness, and eventually to suicide.

Suicide is not always as cut and dry or as defined as we would like to think. Some people simply give up on life at some point in their journey and start doing things that are detrimental to their health and life. Sometimes they do dangerous things that can get them killed. I saw a guy riding a wheelie on his motorcycle for a very long distance on the interstate in Indianapolis, Indiana at a very busy time. I was in the second lane to the left and he came speeding past me in the left lane. I prayed for him because I knew that if someone changed lanes it would be all over for him. Sometimes people use drugs, alcohol or other things to get them to that point of death ahead of time. This can be a form of suicide because it all leads to an untimely death. Some accidental deaths and drug overdoses are actually an act of suicide. I've seen some people who look like zombies, they are alive physically but there is no desire inside of them to live. They've simply given up on life and all hope is gone. The walking dead! It's so sad! Many times family and friends try to help, but they've already given up all hope and refuse to change.

Hebrews 6:17-20, "In the same way God, in His desire to show to the heirs of the promise the unchangeable nature of His purpose, intervened and guaranteed it with an oath, 18 so that by two unchangeable things [His promise and His oath] in which it is impossible for God to lie, we who have fled [to Him] for refuge would have strong encouragement and indwelling strength to hold tightly to the hope set before us. 19 This hope [this confident assurance] we have as an anchor of the soul [it cannot slip and it cannot break down under whatever pressure bears upon it] – a safe and steadfast hope that enters within the veil [of the heavenly temple, that most Holy Place in which the very presence of God dwells], 20 where Jesus has entered [in advance] as a forerunner for us, having become a High Priest forever according to the order of Melchizedek." AMP

ALONE IN A CROWD

Have you ever been in a crowd of people and all alone, even being among your friends? I have! They just didn't get me. They couldn't see where I was. I was invited so that I could be encouraged because of the difficult time I was going through, but the party was superficial to me. I wasn't in a place where I could cross over to fun. I wrote about this in my song, HONEY I LOVE YOU. It's on YouTube and on most streaming services with some of my other songs. Search for Joseph James Singer.

HOPELESSNESS OPENS THE DOOR TO SUICIDE

The longer we stay in a state of depression and allow it to rob us of hope, vision, and dreams, the closer we come to a place of total hopelessness. The first thing that gets us to walk down this path is a spirit of heaviness. *Isaiah 61:3* tells us to put on a garment of praise for the spirit of heaviness. In other words, in the midst of our situation to look up and praise the Lord for He has a way for us to walk through it in victory. Declaring His praise from our mouth is a sign of trust that we are looking to Him for His help. This is to help us get back to where we need to be or to help us get through a tough place. It's like hiking up a mountain and finding some places that are dangerous and seemingly impossible to pass along the way.

Praise is definitely one out of obedience and sacrifice, because we sure don't feel like it at the time. It's not about emotions though and when we realize that we can make this choice outside of the screaming and opposing emotions in our soul, we will discover a truly unique revelation that will help us tremendously going forward. If we don't stop the downward spiral in this moment by getting rid of the heaviness, it is in this area that a spirit of depression and/or suicide might eventually find an opening or foothold to come in to beat us down even more. I truly believe it is impossible for a person to kill themselves outside of demonic influence and help. God has placed within each of us the uncompromising desire to survive and it takes a lot of power to override this. I have spent many years in deliverance ministry and have delivered some from a spirit of suicide. It is a powerful enemy and shouldn't be taken lightly. Anything that can get a person to take their own life is a very powerful foe.

DELAY OF THE DREAM

Abraham never saw the ultimate fulfillment of the dream in his lifetime that the Lord gave him as did some others like Daniel. Abraham waited 25 years for Isaac. Joseph waited 13 years for his dream to be fulfilled. David ran from Saul for years before he became king. In each case the dream matured them, got them ready to walk in it, and prepared them for the call. Delay in the journey is not a sign that the dream isn't attainable, perhaps it's a time for reflection, new connections, adjustment, and maturity to take place.

THE SPIRITUAL SIDE OF DEPRESSION

In the Lord's Kingdom we all have a place, our own lane, and fit into His plans for our generation. Our endeavor is to see everyone find their individual dream and find their place in His Kingdom, no competition, just running their race. We can all do this individually and then come together as a whole, His Body, as the Holy Spirit directs us and joins us together. Our battle is not against each other, rather, the battle is in the spiritual realm. If we can understand this and attain the victory in the spirit, then we have the victory in the physical realm.

Ephesians 6:12, "For our struggle is not against flesh and blood [contending only with physical opponents], but against the rulers, against the powers, against the world forces of this [present] darkness, against the spiritual forces of wickedness in the heavenly (supernatural) places "AMP

There are many things that can depress and hinder our ability to soar and pursue our dreams. One of the main ones is the demonic side of the spiritual realm. The other things are our choices, which can provide and/or open doors to give these evil entities access into our lives to wreak havoc and destruction. The scriptures talk about a disheartened spirit, a spirit of heaviness which I touched on previously.

Isaiah 61:1-3, "The Spirit of the Lord God is upon me, Because the Lord has anointed and commissioned me to bring good news to the humble and afflicted; He has sent me to bind up [the wounds of] the brokenhearted, to proclaim release [from confinement and condemnation] to the [physical and spiritual] captives and freedom to prisoners, 2 to proclaim the favorable year of the Lord, and the day of vengeance and retribution of our God, to comfort all who mourn, 3 to grant to those who mourn in Zion the following: to give them a turban, (headdress) instead of dust [on their heads, a sign of mourning], the oil of joy instead of mourning, the garment [expressive] of praise instead of a disheartened spirit. So they will be called the trees of righteousness [strong and magnificent, distinguished for integrity, justice, and right standing with God], the planting of the Lord, that He may be glorified."AMP

As we read through the Bible, we can see that many things can hinder our walk, our journey, and our dreams. While most of these things are from our own doing, some are from others. HOW WE REACT OR RESPOND IS THE KEY! There are such things as generational curses, generational oaths, and generational contracts that can give the enemy legal right to wreak havoc on certain areas of our lives. One of the clearest examples where I've seen this happen is sometimes when a grandparent dies. Generally, the grandchildren and/or children have been living a good life, and/or things were going a certain way, but shortly after that death it's like all hell breaks loose in their lives. There is no explanation for it because they haven't done anything wrong or different. When this happens, we know that it is one or more of the three generational things I just mentioned. The evil spirit or demon leaves the dead person and transfers to the next generation, most times skipping one generation. It starts attacking with the purpose of weakening that individual so that it might finally possess the person, taking control over certain parts of their life. Genetics is also a part of this process.

Another thing that can happen that gives the enemy legal right to harass us and to wreak havoc are our bad choices. There's nothing like judging others wrongly, unforgiveness, holding onto bitterness, lashing out in hatred and anger, speaking negative words over ourselves, pursuing pride, greed, and power, walking in sexual sins, idolatry, theft, and other sins. In these things we do it to ourselves and then sometimes wonder why the Lord didn't do something to help us avoid the bad things that happen to us as a result. The truth is He couldn't. We gave the enemy legal right to harm us. In His mercy, the Lord doesn't let us have all we deserve and many times His angels step in to protect us from all that is headed our way. Sometimes they cover us under their wings as we walk out of harm's way undetected by the dark forces above and around us.

In regards to all of the above, I recommend reading the books listed in the **RESOURCES** section at the back of this book. Inner Healing and Deliverance are necessary in our walk with the Lord to cleanse ourselves from all of the bondage and control the enemy might have over us. It's a journey and can take some time to do. It's not easy. It takes time and is a lot of work, but how far do we really want to go? Some churches/fellowships have teams set up to help in this. We do this as well when time permits. The more we learn about the enemy's tactics against us, the more we can prepare and overcome. We have certain rights as sons and daughters of the King, but if we don't know what these rights are, how can we enforce them and walk in total victory over our enemy?

Janiece's Story, my wife's biography that I wrote, is a great example of the Lord's love for us. Her life is one of the most traumatic, yet such an amazing journey from a prognosis of certain death to so many documented miracles that changed her life. The book is SENTENCED TO DEATH, DESTINED FOR LIFE. I've written the biography, the screenplay for the upcoming movie, and created a website to help others out in cyberspace who are searching for help with seven videos of her testimony. Through it all, the trauma, the surgeries, the questions, and the seven years of mental health struggles, there emerges a story of the Lord's love and restoration. I have never read of another miraculous story like this, let alone be privileged to write about it. It happened before we were married, in fact, without the miracles I would've never met her and our son would've never been born. This book is listed on the RESOURCES section at the back and on the website as well.

Hosea 4:6, "My people are destroyed for lack of knowledge [of My law, where I reveal My will]."

Jesus makes an amazing statement just before He is crucified on the cross. In the following scripture, He says that the enemy has nothing in Him, no legal right to do what he's about to do, which is kill Him on the cross. How many of us can say that, yet by His blood and forgiveness we have the same opportunity and right to be set free, even to the degree that the enemy has nothing in us either.

John 14:30, "I will not speak with you much longer, for the ruler of the world (Satan) is coming. And he has no claim on Me [no power over Me nor anything that he can use against Me]; AMP

Jesus dealt with evil spirits in healing almost every

individual, but we don't hear about that very often in some circles. There's a lot more to this than just this brief overview and I'll be sharing more in further teachings, speaking venues, conferences, and videos. It is our job as Christians to deal with the whole person, body, soul, and spirit so that we can gain the complete victory in our lives. That's what Isaiah 61 is all about as well as the great commission. Basically, Jesus was and is saying, "I am giving you all authority to take back everything that was stolen by the enemy, the earth, the people, the animals, everything, reversing the curses with blessings and peace." (Matthew 28:16-20) There is a new Kingdom in our midst, and we are the rightful heirs and ambassadors of it, our generation!

John 9:1-3, "While He was passing by, He noticed a man [who had been] blind from birth. 2 His disciples asked Him, 'Rabbi (Teacher), who sinned, this man or his parents, that he would be born blind?' 3 Jesus answered, 'Neither this man nor his parents sinned, but it was so that the works of God might be displayed and illustrated in him.'" AMP

As we see in the scripture above, there is not always a cause or sin, but rather a way for the Lord to reveal His goodness and miracle working power. We could wonder how this could be fair to that individual, but perhaps this allowed the man to be protected from certain things in his earlier years. He gained unusual insight along the way from his blindness that might enable him to do something more wonderful with the rest of his years than had he not been blind. Fairness is from our own human perspective and can be tainted because we don't understand the whole picture that Father sees from His perspective and plan. We must trust that in the end, everything we've gone through will be more than fair and wonderful. Sometimes it's those trying times that give us the strength we need somewhere else down the line. After all, it's His wonderful thoughts towards us that helped fashion the dream He wrote for us. He's also provided a storehouse for each of us for the provision to fulfill each dream. Sometimes that provision comes through others, through divine connections, and sometimes even through a fish. Remember the coin the disciples found in the fish they caught to pay the tax at Jesus' instruction? Supernatural! (Matthew 17:27) Some people unknowingly talk to and get helped by angels.

One of my favorite illustrations is telling people about Pikes Peak. On bright, sunny days we can see Pikes Peak vividly from Colorado Springs and a little bit of snow on top makes it look magnificent and truly majestic as the sun illuminates the snow. But on a stormy day, the clouds cover it and it appears to not be there, like it disappeared. So I tell them that even though we can't see it when the storm is there, it doesn't mean the mountain is gone. Everyone understands that analogy. It is the same with our dreams though. Just because the storms in life are all around us and we can't see our dream, or it seems impossible because of circumstances, the dream is still there. The storms, those circumstances will eventually pass and we'll see that our dreams are still possible. In fact, we might actually be closer to them than when the storm first came. Don't give up! Keep on going!

Pikes Peak and Garden Of the Gods in the Foreground, Colorado Springs, Colorado

Sometimes our dreams seem crystal clear to us, the sun is shining and everything is going well.

Sometimes we feel lost and confused because we can't see so clear, yet the dream is still there behind the mirage of circumstances.

Chapter 5

Defining The Dream

How does one define their dream? Well, most of what I've talked about, the illustrations I've shared, and the amount of brainstorming you've done so far is a good start. A lot of what the Lord has planned for us is already in us. We just need some help in discovering it. Most of the things we don't know is the timing, the actual journey, and who are those who will be a part of our life.

This is where the Lord comes into play, if we want to truly live out the plan He has for us. We can try to do it our own way, but trust me that doesn't end very well. I've got the scars to prove it and I still remember the pain and wasted time. He does give us the choice though. I pray we make the right one.

So, at this time in our life it's time to start putting everything together, look over our lists, and see if we can fit them together like a jigsaw puzzle. Look at our strengths and weaknesses. Look at our passions. How might they fit together?

During this time we will discover that some of the things we thought were for us to pursue weren't ours at all, in fact, they were someone else's dream for our life. We don't have what it takes to run in those lanes and it would end in total defeat if we tried. So many times, well meaning people try to put their broken dreams upon other individuals to fulfill. This is especially true with some parents.

Someone who wants to race at hurdles must be able to jump a decent height and run fast. It doesn't matter how fast we can run if we knock over all the hurdles along the way. We will be disqualified. It also doesn't matter if we can jump real high but can't run very well. We have to look at our limitations from truth, not emotion. Can we practice enough to be able to jump high enough and to run fast enough? Is it something we really want to spend that much time on with the kind of rewards that come? Where is our passion in it? Is it ours or someone else's? What's the real truth inside, because at the end of the day this is what matters the most? Sometimes we do things to impress others and when they walk out of our lives at some point, it leaves an emptiness inside of us because it wasn't something we actually wanted to do for ourselves.

A lot of things become clear when we write them out, pray about them, and not get in a rush. Our emotions in the moment can deceive us, yet it is these same emotions that can propel us to go higher when they are in line with His plan. The Lord created emotions for us to live our lives to the fullest and to enjoy every single moment along the way. Even sadness and grieving are necessary emotions, because they show that we love and they actually have a legitimate purpose inside of us. We just can't afford to stay in a depressed state of mind too long or it can become detrimental instead.

Again, we need to understand that defining and pursuing our dreams is a process in and of itself. I hope that this book helps us begin the process, brings some understanding to the flexibility of dreams, and encourages us to run until we finish our race.

Remember that trial and error is also a way to determine what is for us and what's not. We will find that some we thought were going to be our friends for life will choose another path somewhere along the way. It doesn't mean it's wrong, we just need to understand that some folks will come into our lives for a season, while others might be with us for most of our life. If we can recognize this early in our walk, it can help us more with good-byes and not take them the wrong way. Codependency can keep us enslaved in a detrimental relationship instead of helping to propel us forward into the destiny for each of us.

Many times we might discover that none of the choices we face are bad. Some might be better than others, but they all might get us to our destination. Sometimes we might only have one choice, but as we start walking down that path there might be other choices along the way that will bring more clarity. It's like choosing a path where there's a mountain in front of us and we can't see around it. As we walk closer, we see there are different routes to take, either up and over the mountain, under through a tunnel, or in some cases around it. It doesn't mean that any of them are wrong choices, just that some might be more difficult, have a different scenery, and possibly take longer to navigate. The key is that they all bring us to the other side of the mountain where more adventure is waiting for us.

I use a lot of illustrations to help us to understand the journey easier. You'll find that you will discover some of your own. Write them down and share them with others around you.

As you read through the rest of the pages in this book, take what you've discovered so far and begin placing the most important ones together on a separate page. At the end of this book, you can use this page or pages to write a summary of your dream on the certificate so that you can frame it. Feel free to make more than one copy and hang them where you can see them multiple times during the day, perhaps even as a background screen on your computer, pad, and/or phone. This is your life. Do what it takes to succeed and get to the place you desire and are passionate about.

Dreams are living entities that live inside of us. I don't believe in broken dreams anymore. I believe there are obstacles in our way sometimes that make us dig deeper inside to see what we've allowed to stop or hinder us. Sometimes it's our own thoughts or the way we perceive things. If I would have allowed the breakup with my fiancée after my motorcycle wreck or the failure of my two marriages to stop me, I wouldn't have experienced the almost 25 years of marriage now to Janiece. The things I would have missed out on would have been enormous. People are free to choose whether they want to be with us and sometimes we make the wrong choices, but it doesn't mean it's the end of our dreams or life. It simply means there is another way to go forward, perhaps an adventure we haven't even imagined yet.

REMEMBER THIS! *Ephesians 3:20,21, "Now to Him who is able to [carry out His purpose and]* **do superabundantly more than all that we dare ask or think** *[infinitely beyond our greatest prayers, hopes, or dreams], according to His power that is at work within us, 21 to Him be the glory in the church and in Christ Jesus throughout all generations forever and ever."* AMP

No matter how big our imagination is, His is bigger. He just thinks He can accomplish anything He says, and He's right. Most of the time He's trying to get us to dream bigger and trust Him more. He makes all things possible. He spoke and creation formed, the universe, the earth and everything in it. Look up! Dream bigger! Dare to believe that your Father loves you and wants to do great things through you simply because you are His child.

One of the tunnels on Gold Camp Road | Colorado Springs, CO
Sometimes there's a faster way to the other side | Tunnels

When A to B is not a Straight Line!

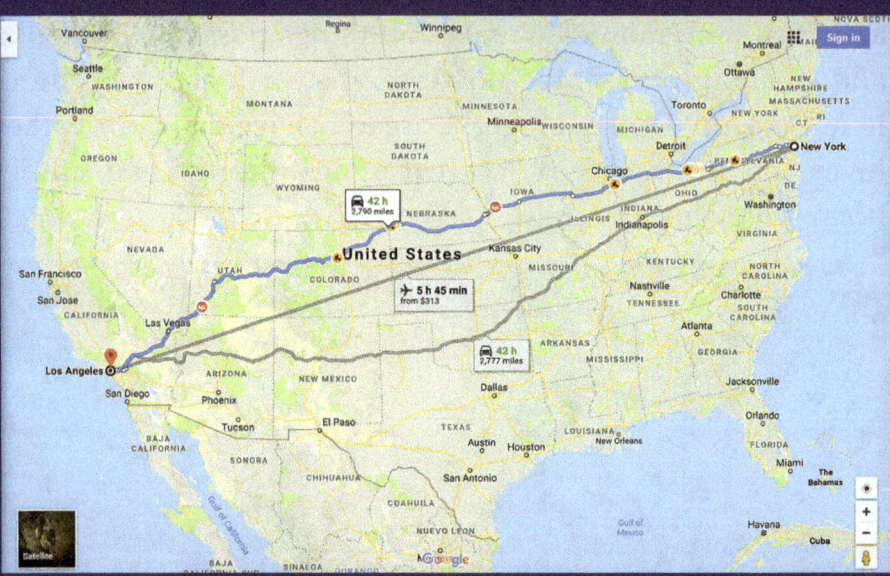

A Journey from Los Angeles to New York With the Most Direct Route Driving

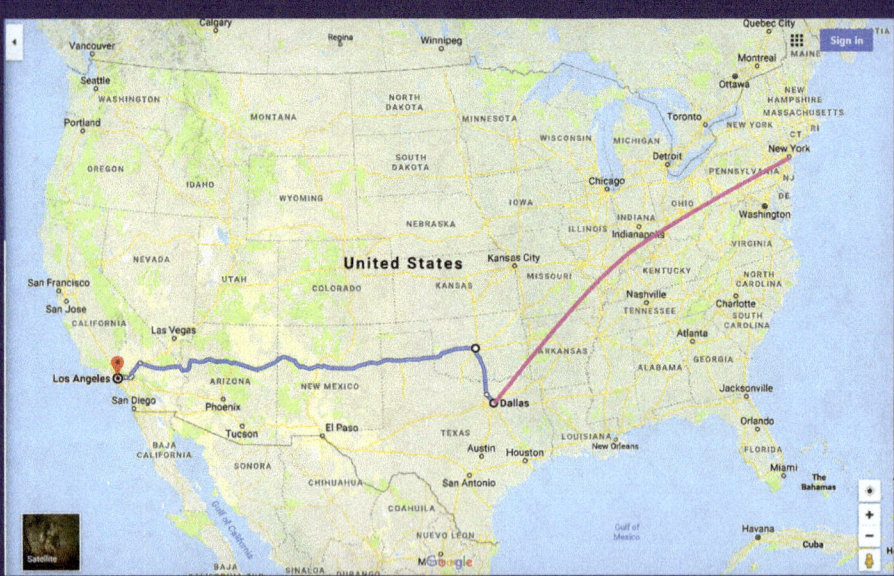

A Journey from LA to NYC and a Detour to Dallas and a Flight to NYC

Maps Courtesy of Google Maps.

Chapter 6

When A To B Is Not A Straight Line

Sometimes we might have to walk a path that seems to be going in the wrong direction only to find that there is a connection along the way who can help us get to our destiny much faster. It would be like driving a car from Los Angeles to New York City. We get to Oklahoma City, Oklahoma only to find the path heading south to Dallas, Texas. We can balk at the change in direction as it appears to be going in the wrong direction and a huge waste of precious time. When we finally get to Dallas though, we meet someone who has a plane ticket for us to New York City, thus saving us a lot of time and driving.

By using some excerpts from my life to give examples, I hope it can help in the understanding of what I just wrote. If one looks at the many things I've done in my life, both in work, education, and projects, it can seem like a hodgepodge of things that can appear like a colossal mess. We used to call this 'jack of all trades and master of none'. To be completely honest that might be true, but it doesn't mean it's a bad thing. I am finding that all of those different areas of knowledge I've gained in my past are helping me in this place I find myself now, putting it all together for the big project ahead. I'll be unveiling it as we move forward and things open for it to come to fruition. Because of the wisdom and knowledge I've gained through the years, I am now able to create something I'm ready to not only do, but to oversee and manage as well.

Over the years, I've been privileged to be in management, sales, a lot of aspects of building construction, some architecture, business, some legal projects, music, technology, web development, graphic design, audio & video, writing, songwriting, acting, and more. I used to think that I was just bouncing around in my life and many others thought that as well, but all of a sudden things have changed. Now, I am starting to put it all together to establish the dream and get others involved in it. It is also beneficial in the writing of my books. If you want to know more about it, just read my ISLANDS IN THE SEA series. You see, the Lord wouldn't allow others to get involved with me until it was the right time. I needed to be ready with my talents and gifts, along with my temperament, the healing of my heart, maturity, and some understanding of others along the way. At some point I'll write my autobiography to provide more details.

My point in all of this though, is don't be so concerned about your past or where you are now, the Lord is more than able to use everything in our lives to get us to the destiny He has planned for us. Yes, we sometimes make bad choices and have to walk through the consequences. Sometimes others make bad choices and it affects our lives negatively. The same is true on the positive side though, and it can propel us further than we can imagine. If we can see this correctly and in the right perspective, it can become a daily adventure that we look forward to discovering every morning as we look to see what He is doing in each new day.

I like to use the following illustration a lot because it just makes sense and folks can identify with it. If you are driving a car down the freeway, perhaps out across a long stretch of highway, do you drive forward by looking in the rear view mirror? Sometimes we need to glance back to see what's behind us, but if that is our focus we'll eventually go off the road and crash. This is true in our lives. We can't change our past, but we can change our direction and destination simply by making new choices and pursuing them. We can take the lessons we've learned from our past to strengthen us in the journey ahead. These are those glances through the rear view mirror. If we allow the necessary healing to come to our hearts, we will be stronger for the journey ahead and not make decisions based out of the fear of being hurt again. Perhaps this time things will work out, but what if we didn't try again? Life is a gamble sometimes. There are victories to be won and some not-so-good times as well. It's what makes us human, not robots. Perfection isn't all it's cracked up to be. Trust me, I've tried, and once I gave it up I really started to live and to be free of what others thought and what I thought about me as well. My identity is not in what others say or what I think about myself. No, my identity is in what Father says about me and He loves me more than I can comprehend. I can't do anything to make Him love me less. I can do things that make Him like more of what I'm doing though. See the difference. We can love someone but not necessarily like what they are doing. It might be detrimental to their life and so we want the best for them. In this sense, we might be a little bit sad, but it doesn't change our love for them. We have to understand this.

We start out in this physical life as babies and have to

learn how to function in this new world. It is the same in the Spirit. When we are born again we are simply babies in the Spirit. It is a strange realm that we can't see with our physical eyes. Sometimes we can only catch glimpses with our spirit, but the more we learn and practice the more mature we become. Falling is natural to a baby learning how to walk. Why would we think we have to be perfect as we begin our journey with the Lord? He doesn't! Soon we can be running with Him if we can catch this revelation. This revelation alone is going to set many free from perfection. The spiritual realm is foreign to us until we walk in it more and more and then it can become as familiar as waking up in our home everyday.

I loved music as a child. My mom had music playing all the time. My grandfather could play the accordion by ear and played with a few others on occasion at his country store. My uncle Roy was the lead singer in a country/western band, The Echos, in the late 60's and early 70's. He even let me borrow his Fender Telecaster to learn how to play the guitar chords in the early '70's. However, I had some strikes going against me that I let win over me. I had some tell me that I couldn't carry a tune when I sang and this affected me more than I ever realized until just a few years ago. You see, when you try to sing and a gripping fear attacks you, it's difficult to project enough to get your voice to sound right, especially to be on key. So, this in itself is self defeating like a self fulfilling prophecy. Without enough air passing through your voicebox, it's easy to be off. This is the same with some instruments. If there's not enough air flowing through it, the sound can be flat and sound horrible. If that wasn't enough during this time with the Telecaster, my stepdad didn't believe in pursuing a music career and voiced it rather loudly. He discouraged me at every turn or that was my perception. So this just added to the obstacles in my way and really discouraged me to the point of giving up.

After her second marriage was over, my mom moved us into town and because of this, in my high school years I was able to play the trumpet, the drums, and all of the percussion instruments we had in band. I bought a Platinum 7-piece Tama drumset and took four years of music theory as well. Then it all went away again as I pursued a different career after I graduated. A motorcycle wreck a few years later changed the focus of my life again and during my recovery my fiancée and I broke up. I still wonder why the breakup happened because we never spoke to one another after that. The communication literally just stopped.

In 1988, at the age of 26 and after my first divorce, I bought a 12 string guitar and a small sound system to practice praise and worship music for our little prayer group out in the country. As I was learning how to play these choruses, new songs started coming to me. I was literally seeing the lyrics in my imagination. I could literally write a song in 15 minutes sometimes. It seemed like every week people were asking me if I had a new song to share. This was very encouraging, but these songs didn't go very far for years.

I kept writing over the years as the songs came to me, when I had a guitar or piano available and have over 300 now. I had gone up to the western slope of Colorado for an extended stay one year and was introduced to a lady who played the piano. She showed me how to play guitar chords on the keyboard and that opened a whole new realm to my music.

Sometime in 2000, Mars Music in San Antonio, Texas had a songwriter's contest. I had written two new songs on the piano when we stayed out at Yogi Bear's Jellystone RV Park in Bandera, Texas. I asked them if I could come in for the next two weeks to practice on one of their keyboards for the contest. This is when I discovered the Yamaha Motif 8 studio recording keyboard and wanted one more than anything. They let me play two songs for the contest, THE GIFT and THIS MOMENT and recorded them on a CD for me. These were my first professional recordings on any level. I was greatly encouraged.

During this time we had purchased a 1954 GMC 35' Bus to convert into a motorhome. This was working fine until we had to move into it before it was complete. Long story short, it was a really difficult time for us because Daniel was just a toddler at the time, but it opened the door for me to learn how to convert the 45' tour buses and motorhomes by working for a bus conversion company in Bandera, Texas. Can you see where this is going? The GMC bus thing didn't work out and we decided to sell it, but I gained a lot of experience in what we would want in a tour bus/motorhome. It also provided a job for me for a season.

I left this job later because my back was starting to bother me more and more when I was working in the bays of these huge buses. I am almost six feet tall, and getting into the bays in all those forms of contortion necessary to install equipment is a bit painful sometimes. So we moved to Dallas next and through a series of events, I enrolled at the Art Institute of Dallas for an Associate Degree in Multimedia and Web

Design. I was able to take a workshop class in graphic design for Adobe InDesign and added that to my knowledge base. This is the software I use to typeset my books and I design the covers with Photoshop. I use Audition, Premiere, and Aftereffects to record my music and create my music videos. I thought I was going in for website development and came out with a lot more. Catch the revelation here too!

As I continued to pursue this new career, the songs kept coming and I started writing a five book series called ISLANDS IN THE SEA in 2009. I just finished writing book five in September, 2018 in South Carolina.

One day in 2011, I was in a church service in San Antonio, Texas when a prophet came into town from Oklahoma. He didn't know me from anyone else, but called me out of the group with a word from the Lord about my music. Basically, he told me the Lord wanted me to focus on the music he had given me, not to give it up, but to pursue it. He said I had an anointing like Keith Green. I was excited because Keith Green's music helped me so much in my early walk with the Lord. So I made the decision to obey. Within three years, we had our stage equipment and I had my dream instrument, a Yamaha MOX 8, which is the traveling version of the Motif 8. Fourteen years had gone by since that Mars Music competition. Don't give up! Sometimes the path has a few twists and turns!

In 2014, I was making more than enough money from my Dallas client to support us and my wife told me to put the keyboard on layaway. I took a photo, placed it on Facebook, and told everyone about it. I was so excited! A friend, who I had just connected with on Facebook that I knew from many years back, wrote me asking for my Paypal email. He transferred the total cost of the keyboard into my account and told me to go and get it. I knew it was that act of obedience to the prophetic word that opened the doors for the next few years to get the equipment and tour trailer for all the traveling we've done.

So, when I say that going from A to B is not always a straight line, perhaps now you get the picture. I'm sure I'll eventually get to point B, but life is a journey on a daily basis and I try to enjoy each moment.

We were in Florida almost two years ago when I saw a vision of a man in a huge warehouse in California needing help. The Lord told us to pack up and go to California. We ended up in Irvine at the Hilton Garden Inn and were using our points because we were low on funds. This was during Thanksgiving 2017. On the third day there, Janiece and I were sitting in the restaurant area drinking a glass of wine. I had been talking to the Lord earlier that afternoon asking him where this person was, because we were going to have to leave the next morning. As we were sitting there and talking later, I looked up from the table to watch an individual walk through the front door, over to the hostess, and then walk over and sit across from us with a table in between us. Long story short, we helped him in some things over time, but he is the one who got my first two albums on streaming music. I told him they weren't professionally recorded, but he said to go for it anyway.

I share these short examples to encourage you. Obviously, there's a lot more to our story, but the part I want you to focus on is the adventures in every day. No matter how hard or difficult the circumstances, there is something hidden in each day that we can grasp to encourage us to live another day. I look back on all of the hard times and I can see that these have strengthened me, given me the wisdom, knowledge, and understanding I didn't have and have brought healing to places I desperately needed. Plus, the biggest thing is that the fears inside are almost all gone. It is a wonderful thing to stand secure in who I am and what I believe. It took a long time to get there because of all the broken things in my life, but it was well worth the journey.

A FATHER'S LOVE

A man looked up to heaven one day, a bit irritated by his circumstances and asked, "Father, do you really love me?"

Father's response was so quick, unexpected, and loud that it startled the man, "Yes, My son! You know I do!"

A long moment passed and the man asked a little more hesitantly, "Why don't you care that these people are stealing from my business and hurting me and my family? I would really like some justice from You over my enemies."

Father replied tenderly, "My son, you know I love you."

"Yes, I do know you love me and I can see some of the ways You do, but what about this area?" the man questioned further as he elaborated on every detail, a bit more boldly. Now, that he was aware he had Father's full attention, he was more than ready to hear His reply.

Immediately, the man was standing before the throne of heaven. His body became weak and his legs crumpled underneath him. The fear of the Lord was all over him as he felt Holiness and Pure Love encompass his whole being. He was also vividly aware that this was the place of judgment. His body started shaking as Father began to show him areas in his own life where he was doing the same kind of things to others. The man, aware for the first time of his sin, began to cry out, "Mercy, mercy, mercy Lord! Have mercy on me! Forgive me! I forgive those who are hurting me. I let go of the bitterness in my heart. Heal me! Please, do not hold it against me or them. I understand now. I can see. They don't know what they are doing."

Father's voice echoed throughout His courtroom as He issued His decree, "Done! Now, I will give you justice. I will deal with the darkness, the demonic forces in My wrath and will reveal My mercy and forgiveness to the ones who hurt you. Now, you go and show them My love and forgiveness."

The man, humbled by what he had seen and experienced, saw that Father indeed loved him and it was by His mercy and awesome love for him that He had delayed justice. He realized that if he had received the justice he had asked for against his enemies, it would have also judged him severely. He received a whole new perspective that day.

"Father, I see You are just and You don't want any to be lost. Thank You for Your kindness to me and my family. Most of all, thank You for helping me understand that You have the whole world on Your shoulders. I only operate in my own little sphere of influence."

© 2012 Joseph James

Chapter 7

Real Dreams Are Not Selfish

Real dreams are never just about us. When I was in sales, I learned that each individual personally knows at least 200 people and has some influence in their lives. When we do the math on that one, it is staggering just how much our actions and our lives cause a ripple effect across our generation.

If my dream encourages others, then what I do touches those 200 lives, directly or indirectly, for good. Perhaps it's what they need to get through another day to keep on going. By them being encouraged, they each influence 200 others. This is a total of 40,000. Let's take it just one more step and that is 8,000,000. So even if it's not that big of an influence, it's still huge if even only ten percent or one percent of that number. Now imagine what that does on the negative side. Look at one song with destructive lyrics, one movie that promotes hopelessness, or even one suicide…

Once we see the big picture, we realize the influence we have on others around us and begin to grasp the responsibility that is ours. I have talked to several mothers with children and a husband who have tried to end their own lives or were seriously considering it. They were caught in a violent, temporary storm where everything was crashing down and all hope seemed lost. What are the ripple effects of that one decision? I understand the storms and have faced the same things, but I made it through and am so glad that I did. Suicide can cause very debilitating side effects on those left behind. Is that what you want? Your loved ones will struggle with the question, "Why?", the rest of their lives and they won't know the answers. Many want to leave this world because of the intense pain and/or brokenness they feel in the moment. They don't necessarily want to leave more pain in their wake, but we have to see both sides to understand the problem. I could tell you story after story from those left behind and the devastation it leaves, not to mention the many years it takes for some to recover if they ever do. It's not just about us.

We are here for a reason. There is a special destiny for us. Yes, there will be times of pain and storms, but if we allow it, those things will make us stronger and help us get to our destiny and purpose.

Did you know that when we work out with weight training, we actually cause micro tears in our muscles? As the tears heal the muscles become stronger. It's the same way with our hearts and emotions if we allow the healing to come. The things we experience in life, including the bad and difficult parts of the journey, help us get stronger mentally and bring a deeper understanding of life.

I want to include a few stories here, because sometimes we need to face reality and have it burned into our memory for the difficult parts ahead.

Suzie, (not her real name), came up to my wife and I at a hotel social area out in California. She and a friend were going to Disney because she needed something fun to do to try to get through the pain. Her ex-husband had threatened suicide numerous times to which she and her daughter always responded, but this last time they thought it was just a bluff like the other times and quite frankly they were emotionally exhausted from the previous times. They were both together when they found him in his van. He had hung himself and they couldn't get over the guilt of not being there for him one more time. She talked to us for over four hours and we also talked on the phone many times and through messages as well after we had left the city to continue on our tour. The devastating effects of guilt were relentless and was totally destroying everything good in her life. She is doing much better today and is going on with her life, but there is still an emptiness there deep inside.

I had a guy get into my Lyft car for a four minute ride here in Colorado. During this four minute ride, he opened up to me about how his brother committed suicide a couple years earlier and he couldn't get over it. He was drinking too much even though his wife was trying to help him through it. I asked the Lord to help me speak the right words because we didn't have much time. I told him some things that broke through. As he got out of the car he thanked me for helping him get through a place he couldn't see out of before. I told him that his brother made his own choice and it had nothing to do with him. It was his brother's decision to give up. His brother would not have wanted him to waste his life worrying and being consumed with the 'what ifs'. He would want him to live his own life and succeed. This was all in four minutes. The Lord can expand time and do what He needs to do to help others through us. This guy has my card and it has the links to my websites. He also has my number should he need to reach out to me. Are we really there for others?

I don't get to see the other side of some of these encounters. I hand out my cards with my info, but it is up to them to reach out to me going forward because I only have their first name through the app. Many, I am finding out use pseudo-names on their profiles so then I don't even know their first name. I value and honor privacy and that is why these stories are so generic in nature.

Suicide is a selfish act of defeat. I totally understand the storms and the difficult things people face in it because I've been there. One could say that is a harsh statement. No, it isn't. It's the truth. Suicide ultimately speaks out through defeat that those around us were not enough to help. We didn't trust them enough to help. The Lord wasn't big enough. "No one can see me where I am! No one can help me! I can't take anymore so I am going to end this pain!" Notice where the focus is, on self. Having said this, I also know there is a spirit of suicide influencing the victim. This spirit is telling the victim these lies. The heavier the darkness surrounds the person and the longer the period of time the victim meditates on these negative thoughts and begins speaking them out, the closer they get to the final act. I wrote a song about the power of prayer for someone who is struggling with suicide. It involves angels in the equation. It's called, ANGEL ON THE WAY. I have another song called, SMOKING OF THE GUN, where the person is struggling with choices to make.

Suicide is not always a mental illness. Yes, there is mental illness, but sometimes the storms of life can crush anyone at any given moment. Sometimes there is a lot of demonic

Real Dreams Are Not Selfish

interference as well. We all have moments and places of weakness. What we need more than anything else during these times are friends and/or mentors to just be there for us. Chicago Fire had an excellent show on this that aired on May 15, 2019 on NBC. It's finally getting out there that we must be proactive in this or we could lose countless others to this.

How can they see and understand what they are going through? They need to be able to trust us in order to let us know. The stigma of mental health needs to be crushed so that everyone is safe with sharing those vulnerable moments without backlash. It doesn't mean they are weak and can't measure up. It just means they need someone to understand the place they are in and come along to help them walk through this very difficult and short path they are on.

Remember Luke Skywalker when he had to go into the dark cave on Dagobah in STAR WARS: THE EMPIRE STRIKES BACK? It was in that place of darkness where he had to deal with and overcome his fears. It was the beginning of the next step in ultimately fighting and defeating Darth Vader, but another thing happened in the ultimate contest. He eventually found that he had a love for his father and tried to save him. He went from fighting an enemy he truly hated to trying to save the person who was bound inside of a prison of hate. There was still a place for forgiveness.

Ultimately, it comes down to the choice of the victim who is caught in the storm. We all have *choices* to make and we do, even *choosing* not to make a *choice* is still a *choice*. Can you see that? Sometimes there is simply nothing we could have done to change anything and we have to be okay with that.

Life happens!

The best thing we can do in our lives is choose to forgive others for their failures and shortcomings. We have done wrong to many as well and do on a continual basis. There are times we need to take time out to heal our broken hearts. We take time for physical injuries to heal, why not the most important part, our heart. We must choose to love one another and help each other to become better and stronger so we can all run our race to victory.

There is a root cause to every problem and addiction. If we can take the time to find it, deal with it, and let the healing come, then we can move on in total freedom. Every addiction is a crutch to push away or suppress a problem that really needs to be eradicated, the root cause. Sometimes people overcome one addiction but then go on to another one because they didn't deal with the root. A tree continually bears fruit until it is uprooted. We can remove the fruit and even the limbs, but as long as it's alive it's going to produce more fruit, bad fruit in this case.

Again, real dreams are not selfish, because they have a built-in mechanism that causes us to care about our friends, family, neighbors, and our world. How can I make a difference? How can I help those around me have a better life? How can we all join together to love one another, embrace our differences, and live in peace?

A blank canvas has nothing to show anyone. If we are all the same, all of us together would look like that blank canvas. No, it is our differences, our victories and failures that make unique marks and colors on that canvas. When we are all together on that canvas and truly transparent, that's when we can really appreciate the beauty in the whole picture, the masterpiece.

Can you imagine painting a snow capped mountain that has no shadows? How can we see where the rocks jut out into the sky? It's the shadows that accentuate the unique areas on the mountain and make it majestic. It is our shadows that accentuate the good things in our lives and paint a beautiful portrait for others to see. Don't cover them up. We need to embrace our weaknesses, knowing that we are on a journey to even strengthen these areas. Others will see how we've made it through and it will give them hope to go through theirs as well.

All bullies are hiding something inside their hearts, some kind of deep wound and pain that they are trying desperately to suppress so that no one else sees it and looks down on them. They have to make themselves look better in order to function and so they put others down and hurt them.

We are not robots. If the Lord would've wanted us to be perfect, He would've made us that way. No, He loves us just as we are. There's nothing more we could ever do to make Him love us more. He desires to walk with us, to know our thoughts and desires, and He wants to share His Life with us as well. What does He really think about us? How great is His love for us? I want to know. How about you? Ask Him! Adventures in His Kingdom!

Manitou Springs Incline | 2.744 Steps | .88 Miles Length | 2,100 Feet Elevation Gain | Base 6,600 Feet | Summit 8,700 Feet | Average 45% Incline

My view from the false summit looking up to the real summit. So many stop here and take the Barr Trail to the side and back down.

After 1:15 hours I made it to the top. What a view down on Colorado Springs and the journey up to the top. Determination!

Chapter 8

Dreamers Change Generations

Dreamers change their generation and sometimes, many generations that follow. I'm going to use a few examples of some and give my thoughts on them.

Henry Ford invented the assembly line in building Ford automobiles. He only had an eighth grade education, yet he built an automotive empire that is still here today. He was a dreamer and an entrepreneur. He didn't need to know everything about the automobile he was building, he just needed to find the right people who did know and place them in the right places in his company.

Martin Luther was a German theologian and monk of the Catholic Church in the 1500's. In his studies, he found discrepancies between the Bible and the Catholic Church teachings. His main challenge to the church was that of grace and not having to work for our salvation. He challenged the church, then had to leave the church under a lot of persecution from his peers. His life was in danger but he kept on. His teachings became the foundation for the Lutheran Church denomination. He found a truth, stood up for it, and changed church history bringing a new revelation of grace to it.

I talk a lot about Thomas Jefferson because his story seems

way out there as an inventor. He truly was a man of patience, at least in this one aspect. History records that it took him over 10,000 experiments to find a filament that would work in the light bulb. The obvious question here is, are we being that persistent in anything we are pursuing? He could've stopped at anytime. So can we! What are we going to do in the pursuit of our dreams?

The Wright Brothers succeeded in creating a plane that would fly. Back then they had their share of critics and it was also very dangerous. They risked their lives to bring us the beginning of air travel.

There are many examples of dreamers in the Bible who I've already mentioned. Because of dreamers, we have gone to the moon. There have been many songwriters whose songs have changed generations for good and for bad. Artists have challenged societies in the things they've painted. Authors have written books that have changed countless lives. Screenwriters have written movies that have changed a generation. Inventors have changed the way we live. Some of these people weren't even popular or noticed while they were alive. Some gained notoriety only after their death.

As we can see from many successful people's stories, many of them came out of a devastating or difficult situation at some point in their lives before the breakthrough came. I like to call this the fire of testing and I believe that is some of what is referred to when Paul wrote the following. Please don't get all spiritual here on me, because I'm talking about the fires/storms that test our resolve in life, those circumstances that can do us in if we let them. This is a great scripture to meditate on though because of its revelation.

1 Corinthians 3:10-15 , "... *each one must be careful how he builds on it, 11 for no one can lay a foundation other than the one which is [already] laid, which is Jesus Christ. 12 But if anyone builds on the foundation with gold, silver, precious stones, wood, hay, straw, 13 each one's work will be clearly shown [for what it is]; for the day [of judgment] will disclose it, because it is to be revealed with fire, and the fire will test the quality and character and worth of each person's work. 14 If any person's work which he has built [on this foundation, that is, any outcome of his effort] remains [and survives this test], he will receive a reward. 15 But if any person's work is burned up [by the test], he will suffer the loss [of his reward]; yet he himself will be saved, but only as [one who has barely escaped] through fire.*" AMP

I know this speaks to a particular truth, but the general truth also is that fires come to our lives. Everything we do or speak is tested, some by naysayers and some by storms and actual fires. So many people give up when things get difficult and it is at that very moment that they need to make a choice to persevere. Five years ago, my son and I made the choice to climb the Manitou Springs Incline here in Colorado. We had been here for a year and a half and were acclimated to the altitude of 6,035 feet in Colorado Springs. We played full court basketball several times a week to get prepared for this endeavor. It is .88 miles in length, going up 2100 feet in elevation, and 2.744 steps to an altitude of 8.700 feet. In some places it looked like it was going straight up. I wasn't totally prepared for it because I wasn't climbing stairs as well to prepare my quadriceps for the climb. I didn't know that I needed to strengthen those muscles as well and that lack of knowledge almost kept me from making it all the way to the top. I knew about the false summit about three quarters of the way up, but it was still a very difficult trek. I had to stop and rest so often. I kept pushing on my knees with my hands to try and get them to go another step for that final stretch over the false summit. Finally, after an hour and fifteen minutes, I made it to the top in victory and looked at the city back down below and the view from there. It was magnificent! Then somehow we found the energy to jog the 4 miles of the winding Barr trail back down off to the side. Exhilarating!

I could've stopped numerous times in my life and not experienced the victory that was within my reach. Many do stop on the way up the incline and go back down. I wanted to experience the top more than the screaming pain in my legs wanted me to succumb to defeat.

Recently, one of my riders was a young lady whose gone through some incredible odds, not only a physical but mental journey as well, and is still working through some challenges. Some of you might have heard the story. For her twenty-first birthday she went out with some friends to party and to drink, legal age. Someone slipped a drug in her drink and she awakened to a paramedic trying to get her to stay conscious. Someone had laid her on a train track and the train had severed her legs. She died three times in route to the hospital. She went through a lot in the recovery and then some serious mental struggles later on, but she is determined to make it through. Recently, she climbed the Manitou incline in just over two and a half hours on all four, and Pikes Peak as well. Persistence! Determination! Passion! Dreams!

In life and in the pursuit of our dreams, our passion to make it through to victory must become much more than the desire of our flesh to succumb to failure. It might take us longer than we think it should, but we can get there if we don't quit. In a marathon, there are winners who come in first, but everyone who finishes the race is also a winner no matter how long it takes. They still get a prize that says, "I finished the race!" That makes all the difference. Are you going to finish your race?

Finish your race! See each failure and mistake as a learning process which can give you mental and spiritual muscles to help overcome those difficult places in the journey. Read and listen to stories of others who have been victorious. Find a mentor or a friend to help in the journey. Encouraging each other is everything. Make a choice to look at life as an adventure, refusing to let the negative overcome you. Life is a marathon and so are our dreams. Some get there quicker and some later, but those who keep on going will finish their race! Prepare to fly!

MY ROSE

There was once a rosebush all beaten and rent,
If one were to see it, they'd consider its life spent;
But along came a man one day, He reached down from above,
He carried it home with Him and showered it with love.

He placed it in some fertile soil, in His shelter all secure,
He gently clipped the broken parts and allowed them to cure;
The plant had seen much trauma, but His love would bring it through,
And then the time to transplant it, in the center of His garden view.

The little plant was honored, it didn't know what to think,
And the many fears that held it back, even they began to sink;
The little plant, in the Master's plan, was proud to be a part,
To bring Him glory and honor was the cry of its heart.

The growing, it seemed slow at first, as the new shoots appeared,
The new life so tender, yet its protection secure;
Finally, a bud appeared, came the time to unfold,
The little plant was all afraid and anything but bold.

To succumb to its fearfulness would cause the flow'r to fall,
To expose itself again to pain brought back the tears and all;
Then it felt the Master's hand and heard His gentle song,
He urged it just to bloom again and to know He was along.

As the petals started opening, a hush just filled the place,
To those staring in amazement at the plant that was defaced;
The one that seemed 'could never be,' was now the Master's choice,
His glory, He has shown us in the power of His voice.

So, open up you plants of His and let your fragrance air,
Let the beauty that's been hidden be seen everywhere;
God is not a mean old man, nor one that He should lie,
But now, He's here among us and on Him we can rely.

The Master, He sees everything, nothing's hidden from His view,
As He died upon the cross, He was looking right at you;
He's felt the sting of pain and death, He knows what you're going through,
So why not let Him heal your wounds and make you good as new.

To My Princess, Janiece
Joseph James
© 1994 Joseph James

Chapter 9

Kingdom Perspective

Society and the world system tries to dictate to us what we can and can't do. It tries to place us in its mold. A system is something that controls. It doesn't allow much for creative thinking outside of the box. It crushes the dreams of a dreamer until the dream is proven true. The system doesn't have room for newbies until they end up forcing a new way through.

Take for instance, the internet! The internet changed every facet of our lives. Google changed the way advertising worked. The dream changed the system. All of a sudden brick and mortar businesses had to change their ways or face extinction.

In the world system we are merely numbers in the grid. In the Lord's Kingdom He knows and calls us each by name. Each of us has a destiny and purpose that He wrote and recorded from the beginning and He wants us to succeed more than we do. His Kingdom will change the very face of our planet and bring true peace, love, and flourishing to the plants and animals by breaking off all of the curses levied on it from the time of the fall of mankind. As each of us fulfill our part, the whole begins to change. We have a choice though, we can try to fit into a system we were not created for, or we can find out who we are and let the Lord open the doors for us where we fit and where we excel. He's already created a place for us, we just need to rise up and take it.

The Lord's Kingdom continues to advance over the centuries as His people stand up and do what He desires. As more and more people catch the vision He has for them, the whole image will manifest as everyone joins together doing their part. The devil's kingdom of darkness will continue to short circuit and succumb, eventually coming to total ruin.

How do we find our purpose and God-given dream? Well, we need to dig deep inside and be honest with ourselves. That is the beginning. We also need to ask the Lord to show us what we need to see and He will. Here's where patience becomes necessary. The Lord shows us or tells us on a need to know basis. In others words, He gives us what we can handle in the moment as we walk closer to him and also according to our maturity level. We wouldn't give our car keys to a five year old to drive, would we? Sometimes we walk closer to that dream unknowingly, because it has been placed inside of us from birth. However, every God-given dream will require His assistance in order for the dream to ever be possible. As far as the Lord is concerned, it's a Father/Son or Father/Daughter type relationship that He desires as we journey together in the adventure He planned for us.

One thing we can do is brainstorm and write down a list of what we see inside of us.

What are we good at?

What comes natural to us? I like to refer to these as gifts.

What is our passion? Is it based on a temporary thing that might be completed short term, or is it long term?

What are some things we are good at, but really need lots of practice or use? I refer to these as talents. They are very similar to gifts but take more work. Let me explain.

Some of the time we can face doing jobs that we think are dead ends, but there is something to be gained in it that we will use going forward. It can be like some computer games where we have to go down various trails to find a power up or prize to add to our collection that we will use somewhere else in the game. We need to make our lives an adventure and it starts with our daily attitude. We can control that.

I am very good at writing. It just flows naturally because it is a gift. I can play lots of instruments but it takes a lot of practice for me to be good at it. Music was hard for me to play in the beginning of this journey. Some people can just pick up an instrument and play it easily. One is a gift and the other is more of a talent.

What would we pursue in our lives if money was not an obstacle? What gives us joy and fulfillment? Would it benefit the Kingdom? Would it help our generation?

In school, math always came easy to me, however, English was another thing. I felt like they always kept changing all the rules. I still struggle with where to place commas, but my gift is writing. So, if you see commas in places they shouldn't be, please ignore.

In the beginning I used my math gift to help me play the drums, but it was so methodical to me and not much fun.

Years later, after writing several songs, I finally understood how to feel the music. All of the music theory courses showed me the symbols and mathematically each had its purpose, but once I felt the music, I understood the symbols even more making the whole that much better.

Because of my math strengths, I could excel at certain industries and trades. Architecture and building are easy for me. I went to the Art Institute to get an Associate degree in Web Design and Multimedia. I didn't realize I would need to rely heavily on my mathematical strengths as well as my artistic side. Many, in the program I was pursuing were having a lot of difficulty. They were either mostly on the mathematical side or the artistic and found it difficult to do both, which the course demanded. We had to learn to write code and yet had to be able to draw and create graphic designs and create portfolios.

Perhaps we want a talent that we don't have. That might not be a problem. Remember the parable of the talents that Jesus shared. Matthew 25:14-30. In the story, a talent is taken from the one who only had one because he buried it and didn't use it. It was given to the one with five. Now, this parable could mean money, but it can also mean talent. What you don't use, you lose. I've experienced this because I was willing to do what was in front of me. I volunteered on many occasions to help people and organizations. From this I gained a lot of experience and new skills that I didn't have before. Perhaps someone else wouldn't do what the Lord had wanted them to do, so maybe He gave me their talent so the work could be accomplished. What about you? What are your desires?

At the end of the day we might have only one talent that we are good at. We don't have to stop there though. If we stay obedient to doing what we can with what we have, increase will come. Perhaps there are gifts and talents inside of us we haven't even seen yet, just waiting for the right moment to be revealed. This is why it's good to try new things and to push ourselves beyond our own limits. We might find something fun in all of this.

Then there are the special spiritual gifts that are listed in the Bible, some are in 1 Corinthians 12.

1 Corinthians 12:4-8, "Now there are [distinctive] varieties of spiritual gifts [special abilities given by the grace and extraordinary power of the Holy Spirit operating in believers], but it is the same Spirit [who grants them and empowers believers]. 5 And there are [distinctive] varieties of ministries and service, but it is the same Lord [who is served]. 6 And there are [distinctive] ways of working [to accomplish things], but it is the same God who produces all things in all believers [inspiring, energizing, and empowering them]. 7 But to each one is given the manifestation of the Spirit [the spiritual illumination and the enabling of the Holy Spirit] for the common good. 8 To one is given…"AMP (Keep reading through the end of the chapter for more.)

We have spiritual gifts and physical gifts that were given to us from the Lord when we were created. Life becomes a journey when we begin our walk with the Lord and discovering His wonderful plans for our life. Remember, He wants us to tell Him our secrets and desires as well. This is what friends do with each other. He wants to be our friend.

One thing I believe that is happening in our generation is

that more individuals are discovering who they are in Him. They are asking Him to help them see why they are here and to help them run their race. It is the job of the Holy Spirit to join each of us together where we belong in order to connect and fulfill His work in our generation for His Kingdom. As we do this we might even be in various places for certain periods of time. We might be around some people for short periods of time while longer periods with others. As we trust the Lord to direct us, we can be assured that He is putting His plan together in order to advance His Kingdom on this earth. His Kingdom will bring true peace and love to this world. It will totally bring a new way of life to all of us, while the destruction of the devil's kingdom comes to its final end. His Kingdom continues to rise as the devil's kingdom continues to crumble.

Some people, including me at one point in my life, are afraid of missing what the Lord is telling them. Trust me, we're not that good. He is big enough and more than capable to see that we hear Him. He's got this! Rest, walk, and fly!

Kingdom Perspective

Beautiful Places in the USA for Adventure!
Go Beyond Your Fears and Spread Your Wings!

Our view each evening from a condo | Ormond By The Sea | Florida

Our getaway to Key West Florida for our anniversary in December 2016. The ocean was like glass. Adventure in the journey!

Chapter 10

On To Your Adventure

Sometimes the adventure begins when we let loose, spread our wings, and just fly. Granted, there are still things we must do everyday, but this adventure takes place in our thoughts and imagination. It is in our imagination where we can go and discover things about ourselves. Imagine this! Imagine that! Perhaps some things won't work, but that's not what we're looking for here. We are on a path of discovery, to brainstorm for a while, to try this and that, and to see what might work. There are no wrongs in this process of discovery, except in things illegal which we want to stay away from doing anyway.

We might not always be able to go on a physical journey, but perhaps there's a documentary film or YouTube video that we can watch to get more information on what we want to research. Some volunteer organizations do things we might be interested in trying. One way to discover a part of Africa might be to volunteer on a mission trip. It might not be exactly what we have in mind, but to experience the country and some of the people might give us valuable insight into whether or not we really want to go there.

If we want to learn how to build houses, perhaps

volunteering with Habitat For Humanity or some other organization might get us on down that road. It could be that the people we meet there might bring us into their business, and/or help us in other ways we couldn't see from the outside.

Adventure is also a time of brainstorming, to see what works for us and what doesn't. Recently I had a young adult in my car as I was driving for Lyft. She was so upset and broken because she had finished her sophomore year of college, but didn't know what she wanted to do with her life or what to major in. She was also saving up money to go back and finish to get a degree. I told her that it's alright to take some time off to discover what she really wants to do. There are so many who have gotten college degrees and don't even use them, but they are paying back a huge student loan. It's okay to be you. It's okay to be different. It's okay if others don't understand you, because it's your life. You can do with it what you want, because after all you are the only one who is responsible for it by the choices you make. There are also trade schools available. These aren't usually as expensive as colleges and you don't have to go through the basic courses so you save a lot of time as well. There are certification courses too. Go on an adventure listing all of the possibilities available. There are grants and the Small Business Association to help with start up businesses. We live in the Information Age and most answers are only a web search away. Take the time. There are many do-it-yourself videos of instruction out there in cyberspace as well, free.

Another thing to do is try out the performing arts. Most folks are so self conscious they are afraid of making mistakes and embarrassing themselves. Laugh at your mistakes and at yourself. Don't take things so personal. We all make mistakes and when we laugh at ours, it gives others permission to do the same. Then we'll find we all have something in common and can go on to being ourselves. It is our uniqueness that makes each one of us special. Those who aren't afraid to stand up in front of an audience and perform or speak are light years ahead of those who are. They are a step ahead in many things because of the confidence they have in themselves. If you have to, take a speech class or something to help. Buy a microphone and practice speaking into it with a small amp and speaker or a karaoke unit. Get familiar with hearing your voice through the system. It sounds different. It's what I did as I was learning to play and to sing. Now, it's natural to hear my voice from the speakers and I really like it. Change the settings a bit and add some reverb. Yes!

There is no competition in what we do with our life. We can get up and walk the path before us, we can lay around and waste our time, or we can simply do something else.

Sometimes our path can get lonely and some won't understand, but that's alright because there are others we will meet down the way who will want to walk with us. We can't be afraid to make new friends and let go of the old. Life has new adventures for us everyday if we will dare to go for them. Meeting one new person can change our life forever just the same way as letting go of one who is dragging us down. Making mistakes is a natural process in life. We can learn from them and become stronger, or we can let them imprison us in fear of trying again. Remember Thomas Edison and his 10,000 experiments. It only takes one time to succeed.

I've been on this planet for a long time and I refuse to give up the adventure. I dare to dream everyday, to see what's new in our world and in the world around me. Who am I going to meet today? If I don't like what I see, I'm going to change it or at least give it my best. I'm going to encourage others today. I'm going to let them know they are special and that someone cares, even if it's only in a fleeting moment.

Touch! It's something many don't do very often, but we all need it. Hugs are the greatest things ever! We need to touch on each other with kind words. We can shake someone's hand without getting weird. We can touch their shoulder if they allow and pray for them. We can look them in the eyes and say, "I believe in you!" Most have never been told this. These simple little things can and will make a difference in all of our lives. We can change the world around us because we dare to change. That one drop, us, in the middle of the sea of humanity will touch every one it comes in contact with. It starts with us. We can have a better society because we are the change. Remember the sales formula. 1 | 200 | 40,000 | 8,000,000 and that's only the beginning. Touch is a vital thing that we need. We were designed to be touched and loved and isolation is the enemy of this. This has been proven over and over again. Touch, but make sure it's okay and welcomed by the other person!

We can change the world. How will we do it? For good or for bad? What do we want to be remembered as? What kind of legacy do we want to leave behind? Are we writing our story and taking notes so that others can really know of the struggles and successes we've had in our lives. Perhaps it will encourage one and perhaps even a generation. Think of others whose stories we've read or movies we've seen and it helped us in some way. Leave behind a legacy for someone to read. They'll be glad you took the time to do it, and will say you cared about them.

Here's to the adventure of a lifetime! Here's to us! Discover His Kingdom, one moment at a time. It's magical because the supernatural always is. The power of the spoken word from the Spirit changes everything in the natural. Everything begins in the Spirit and is then birthed into the physical. Let's watch our words and speak the things we want to see happen in our lives. Faith is the substance of things hoped for, the evidence of things not seen, that moves mountains and can create something not yet discovered.

Galatians 5:22,23, "…the fruit of the Spirit [the result of His presence within us] is love [unselfish concern for others], joy, [inner] peace, patience [not the ability to wait, but how we act while waiting], kindness, goodness, faithfulness, 23 gentleness, self-control. Against such things there is no law." AMP

Walk in fruits of the Spirit. Discover this hidden path and journey with the One Who created everything. From the beginning He wanted to walk with us all day, just like He did with Adam. When we realize He is always near and begin that communication back and forth, we'll never go back to the old ways of seeking that in a physical relationship. The spirit realm will become more and more real and a more complete understanding of it will come become ours. We are spirit, soul, and body. When each part is balanced in the walk, we can become whole and complete. This is not theory or words on a page to me. I walk in this everyday, dependent on my relationship with Father, Jesus, and Holy Spirit. This relationship is my foundation that helps me walk in this physical realm in victory and helps me understand from a different perspective. Death and fear have no hold on me because I know what is beyond this physical realm. My confidence is in the Lord and I know He is more than able to see me through to the end of my book, the one He wrote for me. When I see Him face to face in that moment, I want to see the end of my book, and hear His words to me, "Well done!" That, to me is the most important thing in my journey. Anything outside of that is incomplete.

Blessings to you in your journey as you discover the wonderful adventure that is ahead of you.

Dare to Dream!

Follow Your Dreams!

On To Your Adventure

What is Your Adventure?
Alaska, the Last Frontier?

The Alaskan Highway in the Yukon and the Alaska Range Mountains in the Distance. It is a beautiful, but dangerous journey.

We drove from Texas to Seattle WA to Homer Alaska, back through Calgary and to Florida on our trip to Alaska. I took this photo at 11:30 pm on July 3, 2017. It didn't get dark. Adventure!

Chapter 11

Dreamers Ink Study Guide

CHAPTER 1

What Is Dreamers Ink?

1. Where are you in your belief system? Walking in a personal relationship with the Lord? Trying to obey the scriptures and don't really know Him? Believe there is a God? Don't believe there is a God?

2. What is your state of mind on a consistent basis? Happy, sad, angry, bitter, kind, cruel, middle of the road, etc.?

3. Where are you in your journey in pursuing your dreams? From a scale of not pursuing to pursuing your dream, some heaviness, depression, on the edge of suicide?

4. If you had someone who would encourage and mentor you, would it help? What do you think you would need from them?

5. Is DREAMERS INK something you want to be a part of to help others, not necessarily becoming a part of the company, but rather helping others from where you are?

6. How committed are you to pursuing your dreams?

7. Do you need someone to help encourage you each day to go for your dream, or is your passion keeping you going?

8. What choices are you going to make today that will start changing your tomorrow?

CHAPTER 2

What Are Dreams?

1. What does Merriam-Webster define as a dream?

2. Do you know what your God-given dream is? Do you want to know?

3. Will you do whatever it takes to find out what it is?

4. How many wonderful thoughts does the Lord have towards you? Do you believe this?

5. Are you running your race? Are you in someone else's lane? Are you not running at all? What needs changing?

6. What are your short term dreams?

7. What are your long term dreams?

8. Will you begin your journal and write something in it everyday, even if it's just one sentence or thought?

9. Are dreams rigid or do they change and adjust over time as we grow, mature, and get older?

10. What is the motivation that keeps you looking forward to the next day?

11. In each day on average, are you more up than down, or more down than up? What can you do to change this?

12. Can you accomplish your God-given dreams without God?

13. What is the missing element in your pursuit towards your God-given dreams that only the Lord can provide?

14. Do you want to hear the Lord's voice and His wonderful thoughts that He thinks about you each day? If yes, are you going to ask Him to start speaking to you and have some quiet moments to listen and explore?

15. In the words of the poem, MY CHILD, is this a relationship you might want to pursue?

16. Can you see yourself watching for the little things of love everyday, perhaps a special parking place, or a smile from a stranger, a bird singing right at you, etc.?

CHAPTER 3

Dreamers

1. Read the story of Joseph starting in Genesis 37. What do you think about Joseph in the beginning in his youth, versus who he became after he was exalted to second in charge of Egypt? Did his journey change him? How?

2. Read some of the Psalms. What was David's life like with the Lord based on His revelations of who this God was to Him? Do you think He was hearing from the Lord, even in the Old Testament? Was it a story of love?

3. Do you believe the statement from Jeremiah 29:11? Really believe it? Is it like an anchor in your life?

4. Do you understand the function of the male and female body and the difference between them and our soul? Does this help you understand your role on the earth?

5. What do you believe about deja vues? Is it exciting that these might be actually catching glimpses of what is written in your book in heaven?

6. How long do you think it will take for Father to tell us everything He thinks about us and how He feels about us? Are you curious to know?

7. Are you going to write down the things He tells you? This will help you look back through time so you can see your journey of where you started and the love relationship as it develops, perhaps some struggles along the way as well as awesome victories.

8. Does the Lord desire to give you good things? Do you know you have a choice on whether or not to receive them?

9. Brainstorm for a moment and create a list of everything you are passionate about? What makes you tick? There are no right or wrong things to list, this is just to get you to see it on paper.

10. Do you want to get stronger, to be healed so the things that keep you back won't be there anymore?

11. In the poem, I WISH, how many things can you personally identify with?

12. Because of the things that have happened in your life, do you dare to trust again? Why or why not?

CHAPTER 4

The Enemies Of Dreams

1. What happens when there is no vision or dream?

2. Define depression in your own words. Are you depressed? On a scale of 1-10 with always upbeat being 10 and totally depressed being 1, where are you? Each month review this scale and see where you are.

3. Define suicide in your own words. Are you suicidal? On a scale of 1-10 with no thoughts at all being 10 and totally on the edge of taking yourself out being 1, where are you? Each month review this scale and see where you are.

4. Are your days filled with hope and expectation or hopelessness and despair? On a scale of 1-10 with always being hopeful being 10 and being in a constant state or hopelessness and despair being 1, where are you? Each month review this scale and see where you are.

5. The previous scales are just a guide to help you see your progress and to help your mentor know where you are. Are you willing to put on some praise music and sing with it in those difficult times? This will bring your focus out of the depths into a higher view. Try it. It might become contagious when you see that it's not difficult at all and it changes your whole world.

6. Do dreams happen overnight? Can we just push a button and presto, dream realized? Or do they take time, resolve, persistence, and work like a runner preparing for and running a marathon? Are you willing to pursue your dreams? If so, make the choice out loud now. Speak it out and

keep saying it, day in and day out, until you are convinced. We have to make our minds do what we want them to do.

7. Are you going to believe the lies of the enemy about you or Father's truth about who you are?

8. Are you going to read any of the suggested books that can help you go deeper into understanding who you are and the destiny before you? Do you want to know the traps that are set out to defeat you so you can overcome and win?

9. What is keeping you from pursuing your dream?

10. In A FATHER'S LOVE, what is true justice? Is it fair to all?

CHAPTER 5

Defining The Dream

1. With everything you have written down so far, begin to put everything together and create a special page for the things that are the most important to you. You will use that going forward as you get new thoughts and ideas to add to the whole.

2. Perhaps you can create your own jigsaw puzzle, cutting out the pieces, and naming each one as you place them together. Make it fun! This needs to be a fun place to be, not a drudgery so that you will want to come back to it often to make adjustments to your journey. It's about life and living.

3. Make a list of your friends, family and mentors that you have now. Try to see where you think they are going with their lives. From a place of transparency, see if you can rate them at who might be with you for a short time and those you think will be longer. Don't make this a rigid thing, but one that can give you some true perspective. It might help later on when separations happen, especially when it's geographically. Can you continue the relationship long distance or is that the breaking point? Just some thoughts here to help in the journey.

4. Which of your pursuits are realistic based on what you know so far? Which are impossible? Can the impossible be attainable at some point? Be truthful here! This is about you. No one else needs to know some of this.

5. Are you ready to step out and try some things even if

you might fail, just to see where you are at the moment? List the things you'd like to check out and then prioritize them.

6. All of these things work for couples as well. Take your individual dreams and see where they overlap and where they don't. Then make adjustments where needed. In some areas of marriage we might find that we do some things separately. This is good to do before we are married and then again as time goes by. Refining and redefining our dreams along the way keeps us focused on the goal and helps encourage us as well. In marriages, it can help us get closer in our relationship.

CHAPTER 6

When A To B Is Not A Straight Line

1. Do you understand the illustration given in some of the different paths we might be on that seem to be heading the wrong way, but might end up being exactly where we need to go to get to the next step on our journey? Look back at your life and write down the different paths you've taken and see if there might be something there you can glean, that perhaps you've overlooked. Is there a relationship there that might be more beneficial than you think?

2. Are you so concerned about your past that you can't see anything in your future? Are you looking in the rearview mirror or on the road ahead? Choices!

3. What did you get out of my story? Can you use any of it to forge forward with your life?

4. Are you beginning to see some things in your life that make more sense now? Is hope starting to build?

5. Do you want to be healed and whole so that you can experience all the great things the Lord has in store for you? If so, will you make the choice to get rid of the toxic things in your life that are keeping you from your destiny?

CHAPTER 7

Real Dreams Are Not Selfish

1. Can you see how real dreams are not selfish and all about you? Look back over your life and see where your dreams and wants might have been selfish. Now look and see where others might be included in your dreams, where you both might benefit and help one another. This can be individuals, groups, and nations.

2. Can you see how your life might influence a multitude of people? How does knowing this affect you and your outlook on life? Can you see the big picture?

3. Can you see how taking you out of the picture might negatively affect a whole lot of people, perhaps even your generation?

4. If you could change the world around you, what would it look like? What can you do to help make this a reality?

5. When you are going through a storm in life, will you choose to reach out to others for help? If so, make the choice now so it will help when you face the storm.

6. When you see others going through storms, will you do everything in your power to help them, including prayer? Look around you, beyond the veils of masks that people wear. Do you see anyone who could use some encouragement? Start there. It doesn't have to be a big thing, perhaps just a smile or opening the door for someone, but be careful, I have found that encouraging others can become contagious. That's a good thing.

7. Do you choose to forgive everyone that has wronged you so you can be free of that control?

8. Do you choose to take the time to get the healing you need, perhaps to grieve for those who were lost, and let go of all of the things that are holding you back so that you can spread out your wings and fly again?

9. Make two lists, one of the great things that have happened in your life, and one of the bad things. Now merge the two together where you have lights and shadows. Can you see the image that it makes? Can you see the things you've gained out of each? Paint your own canvas in your mind. What does it look like? Were all of those bad times really enough to keep you from going forward? Focus on the good and move forward into creating a brighter future for yourself and others.

10. Are you a perfectionist that has to do everything right or can you laugh at yourself, knowing you are human and making mistakes is part of the process of growing and maturing? Do something silly sometimes just so you can laugh. You'll find that it actually feels good and relieves a lot of stress. Enjoy life, everyday!

CHAPTER 8

Dreamers Change Generations

1. Are you still a dreamer like when you were a child, just looking at everything in awe and trying to discover the world around you, or have you given up?

2. After reading about some of the dreamers that have gone on to change their generation, has it given you more hope and more resolve to get up and run, to possibly fly high above defeat like the Wright brothers actually did, to feel that wind in your face and under your wings?

3. Do you have the resolve to try an experiment time after time until you get to 10,000 just to see if you can find something that works? How far would you go? Thomas Edison's light bulb project always encourages me every time I get in a difficult place. What about you?

4. The fires in life come to all, some in the form of real fires destroying everything some have built. Sometimes the storms are just mental, but still can be devastating. Through it all we find out what was really of value and what wasn't. It can help us focus more on the things that matter. Can you list some things you need to focus on more and the distractions you can cut out of your life? What really matters?

5. Are you willing to work hard for your dreams, to prepare and do all that is necessary to succeed? Are you willing to join with the Lord in partnership as well as others He has placed around you? No one is an island unto themselves.

6. Make the choice now to pursue and finish your race.

CHAPTER 9

Kingdom Perspective

1. Can you see the difference between the world system of control and the Lord's Kingdom of freedom? Which one do you want to be a part of building?

2. Do you want to be just a number in the system or do you want to be called by your name?

3. Do you believe you can change your generation for the better? How?

4. Are you beginning to see how you fit into this Kingdom by looking over all that you've discovered so far, your passion, your gifts and talents?

5. What and who do you need alongside of you to help you get to your destination? Know that this list will be refined as you move forward and other people move into place.

6. Have you discovered any discrepancies between what you are gifted at, that which flows naturally, and the talents you have that you need to hone through practice? How do these work together for the bigger picture? Who do you need to rely on to help in the areas of weakness?

7. What part does your life play in the whole of creation? What does it add to where there is lack?

8. What is it that you want to do but don't have the talent at this moment? Can you pray for that which you need and pursue it at the right time? Perhaps you just need to find the right person to help you develop it.

9. What are your spiritual gifts? How can you use them to help others on their race?

10. Why are you here, in your geographical location, in this time? Do you know your true identity in Him?

11. Do you know that the Lord loves you no matter where you are in your journey, what you have done or haven't? Do you know that He wants the best for your life? Will you let Him help you and walk together as friends?

12. Are you ready to join with others to make this world a better place to live, each doing their part and bringing His peace and love to all?

CHAPTER 10

On To Your Adventure

1. Are your wings healed and ready to soar again with hope? If not, are you willing to take the time to heal so you can fly again? Janny Grein wrote a song that ministered to me so much in my early life called, STRONGER THAN BEFORE, listen to it if you can.

2. What kind of volunteer work are you interested in doing? Sometimes this is free training and mentoring.

3. Are you ready to go the distance? No matter how long it takes? No matter who it is you need to walk parts of the journey with? How far are you willing to go?

4. Are you ready to be free of what others think about you, knowing the Lord is for you and with you no matter what, even if you have to walk alone without others for part of the journey?

5. Do you know that the Lord is big enough to get His word to you, He's more than able to see you through, and there's no mistake that He can't handle? He already knows everything you're going to do and He's already made a plan to get you through. In short, He's got this. He just wants to walk with you in the journey and be with you, friends.

6. What is going to be your legacy? Are you going to write about your life so that others can read your pages and be encouraged too? Share your life! Share the journey!

7. Alright, it's time for adventure! Follow Your Dreams!

Set a time period in which to come back to these questions. Answer them again, compare, and check your progress.

DREAMS THAT CHANGED THE WORLD
What's Your Dream?
Change Your World!

The Golden Gate Bridge in San Francisco, California
A Marvel of Engineering & Construction in It's Time

The Gateway Arch in St. Louis, Missouri
What an Amazing Feat of Engineering!
The Museum Underneath it is Well Worth The Tour!

From The Author

I never dreamed I'd be where I am today. Looking back, I thought I'd be further along in some areas, but then these other places just blow my mind. If someone had told me I'd have written over 300 songs and now eight books by this time in my life, I wouldn't have believed them. It wasn't something I thought I'd be good at doing.

When I think of all of my failures and the times they were so overwhelming and seemingly impossible to endure, I am truly amazed at the gentleness of Father and His love for me to help me through. My dad left us when I was three and I struggled for years with the father issue until Father became real to me and helped me to understand His love and acceptance. I hope that through my failures and successes written in my books, songs, and shared via video, that you might gain some things which will help you in your journey. I try to be as transparent as I can to help as much as possible.

I have learned how to laugh at my shortcomings. Sometimes I share those things just to get others to laugh so that they won't take some things so seriously. Once we get to a place of complete healing and restoration, we'll be able to laugh more and not take everything so serious, because we will know that Father has this. It was His plan from the beginning, so all we have to do to win is continue to agree with Him on the path and continue to walk with Him every day. Once we hear Him laugh about some things, we'll know that He doesn't take everything so serious either. His plan is going to work out and He would like to share in the fun with us that's in the journey ahead. Will we let Him?

We live in a generation of perfection because we deal with computers everyday. That perfection should never be applied to us because we will never attain it. It is our humanness that makes us who we are. Our emotions aren't based out of perfection, but are fully expressed through our imperfections as well. Robots might be perfect in some ways, but they are without emotion. We can program algorithms to mimic humans, but I wonder how close they'll ever come. Will they ever be able to laugh at themselves, especially if they never make mistakes.

It is my hope that we can live our lives at peace, knowing it's a long journey and there's adventure in every day. Perhaps we'll even learn to extend grace to those around us to be who they are, even in their imperfections.

I am working on a project that will be added to this one about helping our veterans readjust to civilian life once they leave the military. This can be a delicate process, but we can do it. The military is great at developing soldiers, but it is up to us to help them integrate back into society.

I don't know how far I'll get in the rest of my life, but I hope I get to meet you somewhere down the road. Your life matters to me. It's the main reason I wrote this book. I believe in you. I believe that if you remain teachable, having that same wonderment of discovery like a child, you'll see more things than you can ever imagine. It is only those who've closed their minds that begin to die inside. I believe that in many instances, we have zombies walking around us everyday. The appear to be alive because they walk and breathe, but they've given up hope and have lost sight of their dreams. Will they wake up again and live? Who knows!

No matter what you do with your life, I hope you laugh a little or a lot, laugh at yourself on occasion, love as much as you can, try new things even if you fail, look at each day as another day of adventure and discovery. Age is not about the years that's on our physical body, it's about how young we feel. I've met many young people who are older than me, simply because they've already given up on life and their dreams!

Be A Dreamer!

Pursue Your Dream!

Take Others Along With You!

Win Your Race!

Joseph James

Resources

BOOKS

1. SENTENCED TO DEATH, DESTINED FOR LIFE | The Janiece Turner-Hartmann Story, by Joseph James

2. ISLANDS IN THE SEA book series by Joseph James
    a. The King Walks In, Book 1
    b. The Lion Roars, Book 2
    c. Illegitimate?, Book 3
    d. City On A Hill, Book 4
    e. The Library, Book 5

3. DESTINY PATH OF LIFE | The Journey Begins, by Joseph James

4. REPENTANCE by Natasha Grbich

5. OPERATING IN THE COURTS OF HEAVEN series by Robert Henderson.

6. UNLIMITED ANOINTING, WHEN GRACE BECOMES PERSONAL, WALKING IN THE PROPHETIC by Dennis Goldsworthy-Davis

7. NO COMPROMISE | The Life Story Of Keith Green by Melody Green

Dreamers Ink

MUSIC by Joseph James (Streaming & YouTube)

ANGEL ON THE WAY Album

1. *Angel On The Way*
2. *Honey, I Love You*
3. *Fly From Here*
4. *Locked Inside*
5. *The Gift*
6. *Love Song*
7. *A Table For Two*

SO BEAUTIFUL Album

1. *Lonely Road*
2. *Love Of His Life*
3. *There You Go Again*
4. *Crossroads*
5. *Gotta Be Real*
6. *The Stranger*
7. *The Old Man*
8. *So Beautiful*

New Album Coming Soon!

More Songs Joseph's YouTube Channel & Streaming Services!

YouTube, iTunes, Spotify, iHeart Radio, SimfyAfrica, Apple Music, YouTube Art Tracks, Amazon Music, Google Play, Deezer, Napster, MediaNet, Tidal, Gracenote, Shazam, Target Music, Musicload, Pandora, Amazon On Demand

More info available at: Joseph-James.net

Joseph James' Books

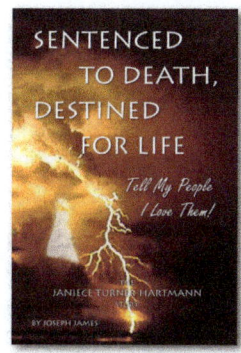

SENTENCED TO DEATH, DESTINED FOR LIFE
The Janiece Turner-Hartmann Story (Biography | Miracles | Healing)

Every once in a while, a story comes along that is too awesome to believe, yet too well documented by so many witnesses to disprove. A story of the miraculous that shatters the voice of the unbelieving and one that compels the reader to go beyond their own opinions and beliefs and dare to enter the realm of life changing miracles!

Into the depths of the grave, destiny reaches out. Through all of the trauma, a twisted understanding of gender, depression, mental illness, multiple suicide attempts, and a prognosis of certain death, a voice is heard from heaven. After all have given up hope, the Creator Himself reaches down from His dwelling place and does the thing He does best, Restoration!

Her story has touched many lives already and has inspired them to reach higher and to believe in miracles. Even those who didn't believe in miracles could not deny what they have seen. He has proven His word again, for nothing is impossible for God. He still heals, saves, restores and delivers today!

Into the depths of the grave, destiny reaches out. Through all of the trauma...

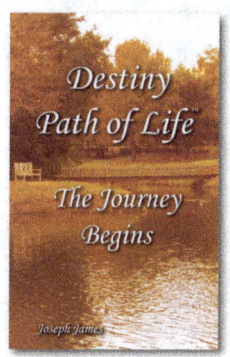

DESTINY PATH OF LIFE | The Journey Begins (Allegory)

Where is your destiny? What will you find when you get there? If you died today, what would be your legacy? Would anyone remember you and why?

Join Bill Solomon as he begins the journey of his life. Discover the secrets he almost misses as he races towards his destiny and dreams. What happens along the way? Discover what he finds as it radically changes his life and his destiny.

"Stand at the crossroads and look; ask for the ancient paths, ask where the good way is, and walk in it, and you will find rest for your soul..."

This fiction book is written in an allegory fashion. Each one of us travels a path in life to our own destiny. It is a choice we must make and there is a reality at the end. In fact, even if we choose not to make a choice, we will in the end, have made one.

There are many voices in the wind and the advice from each is just as diverse. The truth, however remains long after the passing of the storm. It then appears plain and simple, even as the rainbow high above. Let the journey begin...

Dreamers Ink

ISLANDS IN THE SEA | 5 BOOK SERIES (FICTION)

ISLANDS IN THE SEA | The King Walks In! | Book 1

Every once in a while someone is chosen. They aren't the ones we would normally choose for the task, but then again we aren't the one choosing, are we? It usually happens in the night and all of a sudden it is too late. We are hanging on the edge and there is only one clear choice to make. Are we ready? It really doesn't matter, time has run out! We have to decide, now!

Dan goes to sleep as usual, but this is no ordinary night. This night will change his life forever and more importantly, those around him. His choices will affect the lives of everyone he loves. Can he do it? Can he make a difference? Is he up to the challenge? He's just an ordinary man, but now he must be brave, strong and yes, a hero. Did someone say, Hero?

The world is the stage. His business is the launching pad. His relationship with his beautiful art director is not what he expected. His brother knows more than Dan thinks he does. A force in the dark beckons him to succumb to his fear, but another holds the power to succeed. The battle is in his mind, but the war is in the spirit realm. Who is going to win and how will it play out. Join Dan, Susan, John, and Nikki as they get ready for the journey of a lifetime. Has fear met its match? Can love overcome?

ISLANDS IN THE SEA | The Lion Roars! | Book 2

Dan, Susan, John, and Nikki answered the call in Book 1, but now the stakes are even higher. Visions into the supernatural realm continue with deeper revelations and also some unexpected twists and turns. The land they are purchasing for their project has a hidden evil past that threatens to undermine all of their plans. Can it be saved?

Finally Dan and Susan have their wedding planned in Europe and are on their way. However, a simple meeting in England not only threatens to spoil their special day, but places their very lives in grave danger.

The King is again on the scene and now a new creature is heard in their midst. Fear strikes a blow to the kingdom of darkness, but they have plans of their own to strike back. Centuries of planning, scheming and devious contracts are now threatened with exposure. Two creatures in the dark are determined to keep their territory hidden at all costs.

Who is going to win? Will there be a compromise or will they go for it all? It isn't enough that they are just regular people, but how do they stand before royalty and very influential people to give account for their actions? Is love strong enough to see them through, or will they back down in defeat?

ISLANDS IN THE SEA | 5 BOOK SERIES (FICTION)

ISLANDS IN THE SEA | Illegitimate? | Book 3

Dan, Susan, John, and Nikki answered the call in "Islands In The Sea: The King Walks In!" Book 1, and then again in Book 2, "The Lion Roars" but how will they survive in their own city as it is under threat of total destruction? The danger increases as the mystery of the caves begins to unwind. In a race against time, can they save their city?

Dan and Susan are now newlyweds and Dan sees a new vision in the night concerning the new city. Bob gets a warning in a dream in Australia and he and his wife Cindy are on their way to help.

Three dark princes are watching from a high pinnacle overlooking the city. Their hidden schemes over a century in the making are in danger of being revealed. They will stop at nothing to see their plan succeed, even to the extent of destroying the city.

It is a race against time as to who is going to win? What secrets do the caves reveal and what do all of the symbols mean? Was the city really plotted by engineers who were following an evil plan? Does Dan's team really have a legitimate right to intervene for the city and save it from destruction? Timing is critical and so is every step they take. One misstep could prove fatal.

Join Dan, Susan and their team as they dare to do the impossible and save their city.

ISLANDS IN THE SEA | City On A Hill! | Book 4

Dan, Susan, John, and Nikki answered the call in Islands In The Sea: The King Walks In! Book 1, in the The Lion Roars! Book 2, and then again in Illegitimate? Book 3, but now that one-third of the city is destroyed and under water, can they save the rest of the it. The cult is seeking revenge and the dark sentinels have moved to a better vantage point, but something even bigger and more sinister is approaching quickly in the distance. Can they decipher the coded cave system before it's too late and more of the city falls?

Dan's reputation is on the line from false reports and they called in reinforcements from around the country, the UK and Australia, but will help arrive in time?

They had stopped the cult's evil scheme to destroy the city by disarming the remaining bombs, but there is a greater secret still lying beneath the rest of the city that the cult is willing to destroy at all costs. Alex, Dan's angel is again on the scene and the visions continue, but is it enough? The remaining connecting tunnels are even more difficult to uncover and they will require an outside source to do it in time. Can they connect? There's an unexpected treasure just waiting to be found as well. Can it all be done? Time is of the essence!

Join Dan, Susan and their global team as they dare to do the impossible and save the rest of the old city while building a new one on the hill!

ISLANDS IN THE SEA | 5 BOOK SERIES (FICTION)

ISLANDS IN THE SEA | The Library | Book 5

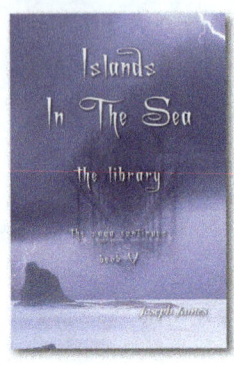

Dan, Susan, John, Nikki, Roger, and Jessica's original team has continually been growing globally, but what three newcomers add is beyond belief. It stretches their faith and tests their courage. They thought they had defeated the cult and their FBI and SIS friends did too, but then the unthinkable happens.

All of their friend's lives are now in imminent danger and all hope seems lost. It was the ultimate ambush and it seemed to come out of nowhere. Danger walks untouched through their front door and menacingly stares them right in the face.

Previously, things were easy with a small team because they knew who they could trust, but now the general public is among them. Their friends from Australia, the U.K., and Africa are back in town, but there's something new in town. It's something that will change the whole world.

Alex and the angels are again on the scene and some new ones as well. Suddenly, three strange lights are seen falling from the sky. The darkness rages.

Join the new team as they discover new hidden clues in the caves and follow the symbols overseas in a race against time.

More info available at: Joseph-James.net

Dreamers Ink Gift Sets

(Buy One of the Sets or Make Your Own!)

5 Gift Sets

    Grade School Ages 8-12
    Teens
    Young Adult
    Adult
    Professional

Gift Set Includes

    Calligraphy/Fountain Pen *(Goulet Pens)*
    Choice of Ink Color *(Goulet Pens)*
    "My Dream" Certificates Blank | 5-10 | Artistically Designed
    Dreamers Ink Journal
    Dreamers Ink Book & Study Guide
    Designed Container/Box for Contents | Designed
        Appropriate to Gift Group

Dreamers Ink

My Dream Certificate Contents

My Dream

_____

As of this day, _____,

"This is My Dream as I see it. I understand that as the days go by it might change somewhat or a lot based on new information I obtain and changes in my life that are necessary for the maturing of my walk, the vision and/or the dream. Sometimes the journey of life takes different paths and turns, but this doesn't mean that I won't get to my destination, it just means there are things I must learn along the way, and people I need to meet who can help me and whom I can help. My dream is not just about me, but to also help those who I meet in passing and those who will become a part of my life along the way. My dream is only a part of the Lord's plan for His Kingdom to be built. He can make the necessary changes to my journey along the way, because He sees the whole plan and knows the best paths for me to take and the special people He wants to connect me with. I entrust this dream to Him, that by His grace I'll be able to cross the finish line in my life and see Him welcome me into His Kingdom upon my life's completion. 'Well done, my good and faithful servant.'"

Signed _____

www.ingramcontent.com/pod-product-compliance
Lightning Source LLC
LaVergne TN
LVHW021714080426
835510LV00010B/990